CATHOLIC MANUAL
OF CIVILITY

Edited and translated by

Marian Therese Horvat, Ph.D.

Copyright © 2008 by Marian Therese Horvat

All rights reserved. No part of this booklet may be reproduced or transmitted in any form or by any means whatsoever, including the Internet, without permission in writing from the author, except that brief selections may be quoted or copied for non-profit use without permission, provided full credit is given.

ISBN: 978-0-9726516-8-4
Library of Congress Number: 2008901212

Printed and bound in the United States of America

Cover: TIA's art desk. Painting by Cesare Mariani, 1888. St. John Baptist de LaSalle teaching in class. This great educator and Saint, founder of the Christian Brothers, was named Patron Saint of all teachers of youth by Pope Pius XII in 1950.

Tradition in Action, Inc.
P.O. Box 23135
Los Angeles, CA 90023
www.TraditionInAction.org

Table of Contents

Introduction 7
Chapter 1: A Man's Bearing Reflects His Education and Virtue 11
Chapter 2: The Proper Way to Sit, Walk and Stand 15
Chapter 3: Order and the Spirit of Order 19
Chapter 4: The Importance of Order in Professional Life..... 25
Chapter 5: The Eyes and the Gaze 29
Chapter 6: Cleanliness and Good Hygiene 37
Chapter 7: The Smile, the Laugh, the Grimace 45
Chapter 8: The Art of Governing the Hands and the Feet..... 49
Chapter 9: The Voice - Speaking and Conversing 55
Chapter 10: Discretion in Words and Actions 63
Chapter 11: Good and Bad Curiosity 67
Chapter 12: Loyalty 71
Chapter 13: Punctuality 75
Chapter 14: Amiability 79
Chapter 15: The Braggart 83
Chapter 16: The Value of Distinction 87
Chapter 17: The Importance of the Greeting 93
Chapter 18: The Family Milieu 101
Chapter 19: A Youth's Relations with His Superiors 109
Chapter 20: Traveling 117
Chapter 21: Proper Behavior for Visiting 123
Chapter 22: Writing Letters 135
Chapter 23: Table Manners Reveal a Man's Culture 141
Chapter 24: Reading and Speech-Making 155

Introduction

This *Catholic Manual of Civility* is based on several Brazilian works sent to *Tradition in Action* by good friends. These manuals were used for the formation of young men in their Catholic high schools until the early 1950s. On a title page of one is a quote from Fenelon: *It is virtue that generates true courtesy*. And then, these words of Pope Leo XIII: *Civility and urbanity in customs strongly predispose minds to attain wisdom and follow the light of truth*. This gives a small taste of the delightful lost fruit that used to be freely given to the youth.

A lost fruit, yes, because the kind of manners set out by such Catholic civility books have fallen into disuse after the cultural revolution of the 1960s, and are rarely found today. The modern man extols what is spontaneous and easy; the Catholic gentleman of the past measured his every act and word. The modern man treats every man, woman, and child equally; civility moved the Catholic man to honor his neighbor with the respect and esteem owed to him, taking into account the factors of gender, status, rank, and profession. In short, these were manuals from the best traditional Catholic school of manners, something I had sought for some time.

These texts needed some work before they could be presented to today's public, so I adapted and updated customs to better fit our times, corrected some historical examples and introduced new ones, and left out some of the complex ceremonials, such as those regarding the use of hats that no longer apply to today's youth. Finally, I introduced comments that my experience as an educator, writer, and journalist has taught me about the youth of our days. My aim in doing this was to give new form and life to works that were completely forgotten, that no one wanted to reprint even though they were in the public domain.

I believe you will find this Catholic manual different from the English-written manners books, which focus on practical matters, usually offering a set of rules of etiquette. Manuals like the early *Emily Post* give detailed instructions on how to eat properly, make introductions, write invitations, and so on. As with most rule books, these readings can be somewhat tedious and monotonous. The contents are more about setting out norms to appear civil, rather than to be civilized. They try to teach a man how to shine for a moment in society rather than forming the entire man and imparting civility as a virtue.

For this work, I did not even consider referring to the more recent etiquette books, which have adapted manners to looser, more casual styles and have modified the rules to meet the low morals of our day: e.g. how to word the divorce announcement, step-siblings do's and don'ts, birth announcements for a single woman ...

This *Catholic Manual of Civility* is simple and unpretentious in style even while it maintains a ceremonial, respectful attitude. It understands civility as much more than following rules. First and foremost, it insists, civility is the knowledge and practice of the rules of good treatment that men should observe in relations of domestic and social life. No, these are not just "company behavior" rules one learns in order to keep a good reputation and get ahead in life. They are wise counsels which, if followed, will impart a Catholic way of being to a youth, maintained at home and in public.

For example, the youth is warned: The uncivil man will be the object of criticism and sarcasm and his presence considered inopportune. And what is the reason for this rejection by good society? Because his external ways of being and acting reveal the lowness of his soul. Good, pure, and ordered customs reveal a man of good character. Bad, vulgar, and sloppy ways are characteristic of egoists.

True civility is a virtue. It allows us to be master of ourselves because it demands an assiduous vigilance over words, gestures, and actions. The day-to-day victory over our defects and bad tendencies is what forms good character, a principal element of sociability.

*

The first sixteen chapters inform the youth how to order his gaze, smile, laughter, and tone of voice, as well as offer norms regarding prudence, modesty, loyalty, and distinction. In short, they aim to form the well-bred man. Each chapter ends with examples from History, the lives of the Saints, or texts from Scriptures that support the lesson.

The next eight chapters focus on a youth's relations with others in his family and society. They reveal the profound awareness of social hierarchy and status in Catholic etiquette that is usually ignored or simplified in American etiquette books. Perhaps it is because even our protocol books fear offending our more egalitarian way of being.

To the contrary, this manual instructs the youth that one of the most important points in the matter of civility is the art of treating each one according to the dignity, precedence, and merits that he has acquired. It is the exact opposite of the boast of the revolutionary: "I don't care who he or she is. I treat everyone the same."

Note this example of the behavior of a nobleman in France, the Prince of Talleyrand, renowned for his courtesy in dealing with others. At a dinner in his home with members of noble society, he served the beef he was slicing at the table. He offered portions of this main course to each of his guests with different nuances of address and tone:

To the guest of honor, the brother of the King, he said, "*Monseigneur*, would you do me the great honor of accepting a slice of beef?"

To the second in stature, he said: "*Monsieur* Duke, could I have the great joy of offering you this slice of beef?"

To the third, he said, "*Monsieur* Marquis, would you give me the pleasure of accepting this slice of beef?"

To the fourth, "My dear Count, permit me, please?"

To the fifth, "Baron, may I serve you beef?"

To the sixth, "Chevalier, would you like some?

To the seventh, "And what about you, Montrond?"

Finally, to the eight: "Durand, beef?"

As one sees, the addresses and the offers of servings of the meat were graduated according to the social levels of the guests. Stories like this raise the admiration of those with the Catholic spirit and help us understand how things were in a hierarchical society.

Such incidents both fascinate and startle many Catholic parents today who have little or no idea about the refined, disciplined customs of our glorious Catholic past. These relatively young men and women are realizing the importance of civility for maintaining the cordiality and well-being of family life, but they are also acutely aware of the lacunas in their own formation. In fact, many of these good-willed parents are themselves the children of the hippy generation, those "free-spirited" minds that cast aside all the rules and declared war on norms and formalities. Now they are returning to the good path of civilization.

It seems to me that this *Catholic Manual of Civility* is exactly what they have been looking for. I imagine it will give an assistance to all, but especially to the men who truly desire to see a restoration of Christian Civilization in the customs, manners and ways of being, which have been systematically smashed and destroyed by the Revolution, especially after World War II.

Marian Therese Horvat, Ph.D.

Chapter 1

A Man's Bearing Reflects His Education and Virtue

Who today speaks about how important it is to maintain good posture, modesty, and decorum in dress when we are alone as well as when we are in public? When it is hot, we imagine this justifies peeling off our clothes and slipping out of our shoes and stockings. If we are tired, we assume the right to slouch on a chair or to throw ourselves carelessly across the sofa. Our bourgeois obsession for comfort has replaced the "grand law of dignity and respect."

The Catholic man should never forget the presence of God, his Guardian Angel, and his own dignity and reputation, which are reflected in the way he sits, stands, and walks.

The Bearing

The bearing comprises the whole of the various postures that the body assumes when we walk, sit, or stand, alone or in company.

The bearing reflects the degree of culture of a person. It is the natural indicator of a good or bad education. It is also the external translation of a conjunct of moral virtues.

All the qualities of bearing are summarized in the dignity of the posture. We should guard and conserve this dignity because of respect for:

First, the presence of God, whose eye is always on us;

Second, the company of our Guardian Angel and other Angels who follow our actions;

Third, our own dignity as Catholics saved by the Precious Blood of Our Lord Jesus Christ.

Now then, respect is born from what we know about a person and the esteem we have for him. Respect for a man comes directly from the knowledge we have of him. A well instructed man, aware of the organic marvels God placed in a living being, has respect for life. When he is conscious of the grandeurs and prerogatives of paternity, he has respect for the sacred constitution of the family. One who realizes the grandeur of the Divine Majesty respects His presence, His representatives, the constituted authorities, and the moral and social order.

In the soul of the youth, respect is an indispensable educating force, because only with respect as its foundation, is it possible to acquire virtue, dispose minds toward the influences of good example, and excite and nourish in youth the noble ideals of truth, goodness, and beauty.

A lax or careless posture is, therefore, a sign of ignorance and lack of respect for the presence of God and the Angels. This attitude translates into a lack of respect owed to ourselves and the persons with whom we live.

A good bearing helps to establish one's good reputation, which each should carefully guard. Because the exterior reflects our inner dispositions, our posture shows both ourselves and others how we are. To the measure that our bearing manifests our qualities or our defects, we merit either esteem or a lack of consideration, sympathy, or scorn.

In the 4th century, St. Basil the Great, St. Gregory, and the future Emperor Julian the Apostate were studying in Athens at the same time. The bearing of Julian manifested the disorder of his soul and scandalized the other students. His eyes were agitated and restless, his tone arrogant, disdainful, and insolent. Scowls and ridiculous grimaces stole all seriousness from his physiognomy; he laughed abruptly and without any reason. These characteristics, revealing a bad character, led St. Gregory to say: "What a monster is being prepared for the Empire!" And St. Gregory proved to be correct in his appraisal.

How different were the Saints! The amiable St. Francis de Sales always maintained a calm and decorous dignity. The angelic St. Teresa of Lisieux possessed a charming, celestial bearing, a most pure portrait of the candor of her heart.

One should never abandon the serious and dignifying posture. The cold weather, the heat, discomfort, even sickness – nothing justifies an inconvenient or vulgar posture because the grand law of dignity and respect far transcends personal comfort.

Good bearing is a sign of virtue. In public as well as when he was alone, St. Francis de Sales always maintained the most correct postures. Msgr. De Camius, Bishop of Belei (France), a very close friend of the Saint, had many occasions to observe him secretly. Always he found him with an irreprehensible posture. Such was the respect of the Saint for the presence of God that he would not make the least imperfection in private.

Chapter 2

The Proper Way to Sit, Walk, and Stand

A straightforward gaze and respectful attitude is important for good deportment. But it is also necessary to know how to sit, walk, and stand properly. This chapter presents basic postures that should be expected from a young man of good education. At first glance, one might think these instructions either so obvious they hardly need saying or too fastidious for modern times. Neither argument is sound.

First, these rules are not at all obvious. Look around us today, and we rarely find a young man following these basic rules on how to stand, sit and walk. We are living in the age where the relaxed and spontaneous way of acting dominates everywhere. Many youth have never learned there is a correct way to stand, sit and walk; on the contrary, they were raised to simply do what they feel like. So it is common to see boys slouching in chairs, crawling over furniture, leaning on walls, and so on. But neither ignorance of civility nor laziness is an excuse to become barbarian.

Second, these rules are hardly fastidious. Rather, they are meant to make life more interesting, dignified, and appropriate for Catholics who take the principles of the Gospel seriously. They stimulate a man to exercise self-control and a constant vigilance over his actions. The rules of civility make the practice of a life of virtue easier, and help to build a Catholic civilization.

Correct Bearing

Correct bearing should be natural and unaffected, without a pedantic, haughty, or pretentious air.

Standing, one should not rest all the weight of the body on one leg, leaving the other slack or hanging. It is not proper to lean on a tree, wall, or piece of furniture. It would be even worse to bend one leg and place the sole of the shoe against the wall, or rest a knee on a bench or chair.

The head should be inclined forward slightly, without moving it from one side to another, or forward and backward.

The feet should be together, at a slightly open angle, and the knees almost together. One of the arms should hang naturally, while the other is slightly bent next to the body. Avoid tracing designs or any kind of geometric figures or lines on the ground with the tip of your foot or a cane.

During a conversation, do not tip backward or forward on your feet, like a pendulum.

Walking

When walking, avoid precipitation when it is not necessary to rush. The step should be firm, without exaggeration. Sluggishness in walking is a sign of a weak, sickly, or lazy temperament.

The arms should move slightly following the rhythm of the step, each foot being placed firmly and solidly in turn on the ground, without making a loud thumping sound.

While walking one should not twist the head or torso to one side or the other; this reveals a lack of basic education regarding deportment. Do not look behind you while walking, nor make abrupt turns of the head or body.

Sitting

When the moment to sit arrives, choose a humble place. If an armchair is offered to you, refuse it courteously. If one insists that you take it, you should accept and sit in it properly, avoiding an attitude of softness or laziness.

It is not proper to fall into the chair, or to rise from it abruptly. Once seated, do not lean the body forward or slump into the back of the chair.

The feet should set perpendicular to the ground, the knees almost together. It would be uncivil to stretch out your legs, or place one foot on top of the other. If you are in special company, do not cross your legs. Among friends of the same level, it is normal to do so.

It is yet more unpardonable to put your hands under your legs or on your shoes, hold one knee with your hands crossed in front of it, or take other such positions.

Once seated, take care to not fidget or stir anxiously on the edge of the seat. Your arms should not be extended over the arms of the chair or bench; also, do not place them over or behind the back of the neighboring chair.

When standing or seated, do not hold your cane or umbrella; these objects should be placed in an appropriate place.

In the presence of another person, do not run your hand through your hair, put your fingers in your ears or nose, scratch your face or any part of the body, put your hand in your jacket or trouser pockets. These habits are reprehensible.

Remember that a fool does not sit, stand, rise, or walk like an intelligent man.

Good Manners Count

Colbert was the son of a cloth merchant who rose to be the Minister of Finance of Louis XIV, King of France. Because he was from a humble family, he was obliged to achieve that high dignity by means of work and merit. Here you will see how good manners served him at the beginning of his brilliant career.

Already at that time, places in profitable business establishments were very coveted and often attained by a word from persons of influence or letters of recommendation. Colbert was 12-years-old when he had occasion to apply for a promising place in a commercial business. But there was only one vacancy to be filled and many applicants. Almost all brought letters of recommendation, and Colbert had none.

To determine the most suitable candidate, the manager of the business decided to make some tests. First, he invited all the applicants to appear in his office at a certain time. When he opened the door, the boldest youths pushed forward into the room and chose the best seats. Young Colbert, like several others, remained standing, hat in hand, waiting outside until someone indicated he should enter and showed him a place to sit.

The manager had purposely left open the door of an adjoining room, where there were some papers on the floor. No one except Colbert rose from his chair in order to pick them up and give them to one of the employees of the firm.

The manager then left the office for some minutes. Only Colbert had the courtesy to rise as a sign of respect when he returned.

After these tests, the manager hesitated no longer and chose young Colbert to fill the one existing vacancy.

Chapter 3

Order and the Spirit of Order

This is an important theme often overlooked in manners books. The topic of order is especially important for counter-revolutionaries, given that the word *revolution* means to upset something that is in order, and to establish disorder in its place. It makes sense that a counter-revolutionary man will respect and love order in his daily life. For this, he needs to develop the habit of order from the time he is young. Good parents and teachers will help him to follow a schedule, and insist that he maintain order in his person and belongings. Later, he will reap the good fruit that comes from having the spirit of order in his life.

Order expresses a regulated life

Order is the practical expression of a regulated life. The spirit of order is the inclination – innate or acquired – toward this regularity.

The spirit of order is a most precious quality. It should be included as one of the most indispensable attributes of a man in his private as well as social life, because it extends itself beneficially to our personal actions as well as our relations with our neighbor.

This most beautiful attribute exercises a decisive influence over a man's success in life. Order gives value to our talents and qualities, and makes them fecund, just as its absence renders our highest aspirations barren and our best gifts futile.

Order is economy of time and money. It allows us to give a better quality and greater quantity of results in both our material and intellectual labors because with it, we take full advantage of time, avoiding dawdling, delay, and doubt.

Disorder is the dissipation of time and talent, the ruin of all the advantages of organization.

With regard to order, this most valuable attribute, let us observe a man in the various stages of his life.

The Student

The student who despises the supreme rule of order – "A place for everything and everything in its place" – lives in an interminable round of irritation and turmoil. At the end of the day, when he returns from school, he throws his book bag and books anywhere instead of placing them in the proper place, which is always the same.

So there are his books – on a bench, a chair, the top of a bed or bureau, perhaps in the kitchen or on the porch.

If another person without the spirit of order happens upon it, the book bag is tossed aside, perhaps kicked out of the way, and ends up in another place. This could just be the beginning of its travels. In the kitchen, it becomes stained, on the porch, it is soiled; in the hall, it is stepped on.

When it is time to study, the boy can be heard shouting, "Where is my book bag? Who has taken my books?" With all this comes a loss of time, irritation, and bad moods.

Then, we open this famous book bag, and we see that nothing is in its proper place: pens, pencils, books, notebooks, rulers – everything is mixed up. The disorder is so great that to find his eraser, he has to empty its whole contents.

Now, let us look at the books and notebooks: here one notes the same phenomena. Nothing is clean; there are cartoons and ridiculous scrawling on the covers and even on some pages.

His homework also lacks order. The writing is not on the lines, the letters are poorly formed, the periods, commas, and punctuation marks seem to have been spilled into the text like pepper on macaroni, everything here and nothing there.

A book bag and desk are, in fact, like a world in miniature, reflecting the owner, as well as telling much about the school, lessons, and method of teaching. To the question of whether or not a person is ordered or disordered, his desk will respond, answering with either praise or criticism. Further, this response will be true for many years to come. It predicts the way of life of this boy, the man of tomorrow, more surely than could any palm reader or fortune teller.

One can see that from one's early years, it is necessary to have the habit of order in the treatment of one's books, notebooks, and articles of clothing. The habit of order accompanies a man throughout his whole life. It is as inseparable from him as his very name.

The Young Man

The moment necessarily arrives when the boy takes on the responsibilities of life, becoming the master of what he will do and how he organizes his time.

When he is faithful to the recommendations of his first masters and educators, he knows how to arrange his schedule and rule of life, which directs all his interests. There are four parts to this daily schedule, which begins with morning prayer. *The first* deals with his daily and weekly religious practices; *the second* pertains to his occupation and method of work; *the third* concerns his family relations, and *the fourth,* his social relations. That is, he orders his life, giving priority to the essential and most important.

The spirit of order acquired during his primary education guarantees him success. By means of this regime of order, he works methodically and produces fruitful works. Following it, he will easily fulfill his duties. His conscience, always at peace, will secure for him a profound happiness, the sweet fruit of subjection to the discipline of duty.

On the contrary, how sad it is to see a young man without the spirit of order and discipline, who is the slave to incessant changes and whims of the moment. Rising is a new sacrifice each day, since he is the last person in the house to bed. The morning hours, splendid, lucid, and most precious, are lost or wasted on frivolities. His room also reflects the lack of order: books and magazines in piles on the floor, shoes and clothing left here and there, a picture of the disordered customs of his life.

His frequent tardiness at the family table deprives his parents of the warm convivium that makes the intimacy of the home so salutary. Frequent entertainment – computer games, watching TV, movies, etc. – rob part of his days and nights. His time for going to bed is irregular.

With a heavy heart, his father sees a future ahead without bright hopes; his mother grieves, knowing her son does not have the habits that lead to a life of virtue.

Poor physical health and moral health are the sad result of a life without order.

The spirit of order should be instilled early

Order is, therefore, of the highest importance. It should be practiced from an early age. Certain persons have the spirit of order instinctively. Entering a room, they cannot bear to see objects strewn on the ground; they pick them up and put them in their proper places. A cupboard or drawer is open; they close it. They have a sense of proportion and a genius for classification, assisted by a good memory.

An ordered man is a precious help in a family. All have recourse to him, because he knows where the letters, the books, the paid bills, the tools, the utensils are.

A young man should be accustomed from his earliest years to order and method in life and regularity in work. There should be no clutter and confusion in his pockets, drawers, closets, and work desk. Everything should be in its proper place. He extends this spirit of order to his computer, arranging his files so he can find what he is looking for when he needs it.

He should periodically clear out the papers and objects that fill the corners of certain rooms. What a mountain of useless items can collect in a closet or on a work table when it becomes the place to throw newspapers, magazines, books, letters, and various odds and ends.

The ordered youth follows a routine every night, washing himself, brushing his teeth, laying out his clothes for the next day in a convenient place. Before retiring, he kneels to say his night prayers.

Order is attainable by all

Fortune and poverty are distributed by God as He pleases. Some of us, through no merit of our own, enjoy the goods of this earth. Others may have to bear the hardship of penury.

In general, it is fairly easy to manage a house when a person is wealthy enough to have a large staff of servants. But it is more difficult and meritorious to establish order, cleanliness, and hygiene in situations of poverty. There is no doubt that the Holy Family of Nazareth found itself in the second case. It was not wealthy. Nonetheless, order, cleanliness, and contentment shone in every corner.

Here is another case. On April 18 the Church celebrates the feast of Blessed Marie of the Incarnation, who was the spouse of a wealthy gentleman Monsieur Pierre Acarie. When her husband encountered difficulties of a political nature, his family estate was seized and he was exiled from Paris. Creditors entered into the house of the family and took everything, the furniture, clothing, and dishware. They did not even leave a chair to sit on.

Amid such sorrow and abandonment, this strong, devout woman did not become discouraged. Placing all her hope in God, she worked assiduously, reduced the expenses to the most indispensable, put the sons to work, inspired the confidence of all, and in the end maintained an honest family home and respected name.

Later she entered a convent, introduced the Carmelites into France, and died a saint.

Order is the virtue of the rich, and the wealth of the poor. Where a schedule and order are lacking, the voice of duty is not heard.

Chapter 4

The Importance of Order in Professional Life

This chapter extends the principles of order to the business life. It stresses the value of instilling a sense of order from the earliest age for several reasons:

First, because it forms work habits that assure success in one's undertakings in life;

Second, and more important, if a man maintains order in material things around him, he will have the propensity to maintain order in his soul and ideas. Ordered thinking will influence his way of being.

Instead of being unkempt, disorganized, and unmethodical, a man who loves order will have a calm and disciplined spirit. He will be capable of doing many and great things, especially if he is motivated by high ideals and love of God. How many "dreamers" plan great feats of counter-revolutionary action, but never accomplish anything because, lacking the spirit of initiative and order, their grand plans never materialize into concrete actions.

Order is the key to success

Order is what gives life and prosperity to every undertaking; disorder is the ruin and death of an enterprise.

In business and industry, order is not just a virtue, but an essential condition. What will be the fate of a business where there is no order in the bookkeeping? Here we are dealing not just with appearances of a more or less exact order, but rather the strictest precision. A log or accounts book should be very exact: to forget an inscription, to write a bookkeeping entry in the wrong place, to miscarry figures and leave out numbers is more serious than mere negligence. It is a shortcoming that can have fatal consequences: loss of credit, downfalls, decadence, and finally, destruction. Business and industry cannot admit or tolerate the lack of order.

In the office

We enter a work place where various employees are working. The work space is carefully divided, each station with its requisite machines and equipment. Every employee has within reach the necessary tools and parts, ordered by section, group, size, and quality. No time is lost in looking for items, because each thing is in its place. Order and diligence reign in every section. For this reason, the work is well done, abundant, and gainful.

On a certain day, a new worker enters the office. He is a young man eager to work, energetic, honest, and able. However he does not have the spirit of order. He uses any item within reach; he borrows equipment from his companions and then forgets to return them to their owners. In his work space, things gather and pile up in cluttered heaps, a situation that affects his co-workers who cannot find their things.

In several weeks, the office is in disorder. In the storeroom, everything is in disarray. The other workers are missing various work tools. This is the moment when discussions, arguments, and reciprocal accusations begin. One becomes irritated with another, time is lost, and the bickering is endless. It is impossible to continue in this way. Either the new worker must change his ways or he must leave. This measure is judicious, because a disordered man harms all those with whom he works.

In public services

In services related to public health, a meticulous and absolute order is imperative. In this branch, a careless order or poorly written medical prescription can have disastrous consequences. A sick or wounded man depends upon the promptness, order, and diligence of caregivers and their assistants.

How many times in accidents and catastrophes, the assistance is less than what it should be because the material needed at that precise moment was missing or misplaced. A key was not in its spot; a medicine could not be found; a surgical tool was lost and not replaced, and so on. A lack of order in any branch of public service can cause serious problems.

In public administration, order is not just a professional quality, but a pillar of national life. Disorder in public services can be a primary cause of the downfall of administrations, and even countries. There has to be order in finances, the army and police, educational and justice systems, and so on.

Disorder generates bad ideas and ridicule

Disorder in the government of material things easily generates a disorder or lack of government in ideas. The person who is accustomed to the spirit of order is generally calm, serene, and prompt, finishing his work at the right time. On the other hand, the disordered person is ordinarily nervous, agitated, late with his work, and everything is badly done.

Further, disorder generates ridicule, because it is ridiculous to see a man rummaging for the objects he needs, turning out his pockets, questioning others, running here and there. Who does not laugh to see the disheveled passenger who arrives at the station, flustered and panting, dropping his jumbled bags, his eyes bulging, his face flushed and wet with perspiration, only to find the train has already left? He is the victim of his own lack of order.

Order is required for an accomplished life

A life directed by the spirit of order is rich in useful works. The illustrious geologist George Cuvier, one of the most influential figures in science in the early 19th century, cultivated the spirit of order in every aspect of his work and life. He had a job marked for each hour, a particular cabinet for each type of work, and in this cabinet he kept everything necessary for that work: the specimens, books, sketches, etc. This custom of constant order permitted him to realize the incomparable works that made him famous in his field.

A 19th century statesman who accomplished great reforms in every branch of government and all the public institutions was Ecuadorian president Gabriel Garcia Moreno. In his daily rule of life, he made this notation: "Every morning before beginning my work, I will write down what I have to do, being very careful to distribute my time well, to give myself only to useful and necessary business, and to continue it with zeal and perseverance."

Let us imitate a similar order so that our lives will produce abundant fruit. Let us assign a place to each object. Let us always return each object to its proper place, and let us carry out each work at the appointed hour and in the time scheduled for it.

Chapter 5

The Eyes and the Gaze

Our eyes reveal who and what we are. This chapter sets out the three responsibilities a young man has in the care of this feature.

First, a man should learn to read the faces of his neighbor so that he can respond properly to them. If he does this, he can learn to not provoke a person who is in a bad mood or angry. He can avoid relations with those who are furtive or devious. He will be inspired by the honesty and candor of the good friend. In short, a man has the duty to become a "face-reader." He should also maintain an amiable and forthright expression before others. A young man should master himself and his expression. How disagreeable to everyone is the sulking, pouting face of the spoiled boy or the moody face of the temperamental youth.

This first point is particularly interesting for us as Americans who tend to believe that faces and gazes do not reflect the internal disposition of a person. We should note carefully how common and normal it is for other peoples to consider the analysis of the physiognomy as one of the most elementary things a young man should learn to do.

Second, we have a natural duty to keep our eyes physically clean and guard them from harm.

Third, morally speaking, what we permit the eyes to see has an effect on what we think. Our Lord clearly taught that a man can sin, even mortally, with his eyes if he looks at persons or pictures that evoke impure thoughts. Men must practice custody of the eyes from the time they are boys. Good parents and teachers must teach youth to avert the eyes from immoral pictures, bad scenes on media screens, and things that can lead to sinful thoughts.

The nobility of the human face

Of all the parts of the human body, the face is certainly the most distinguished, noble, beautiful, and expressive. The face is the part of the human body that expresses externally the sentiments and feelings of a man. On it one finds a painting of the interior man: his spirit, will, sentiments, feelings, emotions, sorrows, and pleasures, as well as his virtues and vices.

Impressions and age transform the physiognomy, which can be described as the general expression of the face. One same face serves for laughter and weeping; fury is replaced by the smile; a shocking or offensive word brings a flush to the cheek, and intense moral agony raises a sweat. A deep sadness covers the face with a somber veil. Happiness illuminates it, a smile brightens it like a ray of light. The eyes shine with pleasure or anger, with contentment or hope.

All these transformations are direct reflections of states of soul, a definite translation of a man's feeling, thinking, and state of conscience. No telegraph system ever possessed such varied and rapid signals.

From this it follows that in dealing with others, every person should be a face-reader, that is, he should know how to read and interpret the signs stamped on the physiognomies of those with whom he lives and works.

Another duty that living with others imposes on us is to offer to others an amiable and benevolent physiognomy, wherein others read cordiality and affability. A face that attracts or repulses others does not depend on the regularity or natural lines of our features; rather, it relies on the expression of goodness or harshness that we project on our faces.

Repulsive physiognomies are those that lack an interior, intellectual or moral serenity, or reflect an unbalanced or frivolous state of soul. For example, it is unsettling to see a person maintain a dark somber air during an amusing narrative, or have a smiling cheerful demeanor when listening to the story of a disaster or sorrowful event.

The eyes are the light of the body

The eyes are the most noble and precious organs that embellish man. With them we enjoy an empire of unlimited extension; we can contemplate both the infinitely grand using a telescope and the infinitely small by means of a microscope, both respectively immense and marvelous.

The eyes – and its visual memory – are the strongbox in which we store the physiognomies of our loved ones, as well as the treasured panoramas and landscapes of our homeland. Nothing translates the thinking and spirit of a man as well as the eyes. They animate and illuminate the features; they are the most distinguishing and personal characteristic of a man.

When we cannot observe the eyes, everything becomes undecipherable in a physiognomy. When a man hides his eyes behind dark glasses, he becomes enigmatic. To the candid, upright soul, he appears to be hiding a reprehensible aspect of his character or some such defect.

In every person, in childhood above all, the clarity of the gaze is the reflection of the purity of the soul. In the gaze of a mother, a whole history of maternal love is condensed and summarized. From the eyes come tears, unequivocal signs of strong emotion. Among the Hebrews and Arabs, the eye means fountain; in fact, the eyes pour forth streams of tears, torrents of anger, or a flood of goodness.

There are eyes that are furtive, hard, and dry. Others are sincere, limpid, amiable, and captivating. Some irritate, others please. Some repel, others attract and encourage. The human gaze has an indescribable influence and power. The image of the gaze of a father and mother, for example, will remain impressed on the memory of the child throughout his whole life. The sweet light of their eyes can direct children on the correct road. Fortunate the child who finds such a gaze in the bitter hours of adversity and temptation! How many men were saved from despair by the understanding he felt from a friendly gaze.

The eyes have a powerful influence to captivate and seduce or repel and terrorize, to punish or reward, to animate or discourage. With his gaze a man dominates wild beasts, tames lions, and subjugates the ferocity of tigers.

The duty to care for these precious tools

The first natural duty is, then, to treat our eyes well. Every instrument, above all when it is delicate, needs to be kept clean to be preserved in a good state. Now, we have only one pair of eyes; therefore, they should be treated with the greatest care and consideration.

One should not read or write without sufficient light in the room. Youths are frequently careless in this point; later they lament their imprudence because, even in this world, everyone has to pay the consequences of actions that transgress the wisely established natural laws.

Likewise, too much light, just like sudden and too prolonged flashes, is harmful to the eyes. Those who watch too much television, frequent the movie theaters, or use professional equipment that strains the eyes can easily suffer eyestrain or other more serious visual impairments.

Eyestrain, headaches, and blurred vision can also be caused by long hours at the computer. Wise parents will restrict the use of computers for children. The youth should establish good habits when using the computer: setting the monitor, desk, and chair at comfortable distances and heights, sitting straight in the chair with the shoulders relaxed and lower back supported, modifying the lighting to eliminate glare and harsh reflections, and resting the eyes periodically. It is advisable to get up, stretch your back and neck and look around every 20 minutes.

It is not enough to protect the eyes from these external dangers. Often we can suffer serious eye problems because of a lack of hygiene. We should never touch or wipe these delicate organs with dirty hands, fingers, cloths, or handkerchiefs.

Respect and purity

There is another extremely important care we should take, that is, to always make good use of our eyes. The supreme law is to always keep guard over them within the limits of Catholic modesty. Our eyes should not rest on objects that awaken bad thoughts.

Let our eyes serve us to observe and admire the grand spectacles of nature and the heavens, the qualities and the prodigious variety of minerals, plants, and animals.

We should ponder even more the gazes of our parents, reading in them their tenderness and love; at times we can also read the displeasure that our faults cause them. Their severe gazes serve to correct us and keep us from going astray.

The eyes of a good son express love, reverence, and fidelity, just as the eyes of a bad son reveal the lie, disloyalty, and a bad state of soul.

Instead of furtive and deceitful gazes, let us seek to have an open, frank physiognomy, one that is filled with compassion for a suffering neighbor, submissive and respectful toward the elderly, and at the same time always firm and resolute against the enemies of God and country.

The eyes are the windows of the soul; for the incautious, spiritual death enters through these windows. It is necessary to be very vigilant over the sense of sight, insomuch as gluttony of the eyes, as Bossuet says, is a vice that can never be satiated and has no boundaries or bottom. If one does not have custody over the eyes, they become infernal hooks that snatch the soul without fail and make it fall into sin.

We need only recall the wife of the Pharaoh, Puttifar, who tried to seduce Joseph; the accusers of the chaste Suzanna; the imprudence of the gaze of David on Bathsheba and its sad consequences.

The eyes are the mirror of the soul. Attila, the ferocious king of the Huns, had small, restless, fiery eyes, athirst for pillage and blood. In Mantua, he was subjugated by the serene and grave gaze of St. Leo the Great.

Recall also how the tender gaze of the Divine Savior opened a perennial fountain of tears of contrition and salvation in the unfaithful Peter.

The most beautiful spectacle in the world

The face of the innocent man is so handsome that an ancient author correctly affirmed that the most beautiful spectacle in the world was the face of a young man of 20 years who knew how to preserve his innocence.

Here follows the physical description of Our Lord's face and demeanor from an original letter of the Roman official Publius Lentullus in a report to the Senate:

"There appeared in these our days a man of the Jewish Nation of great virtue, named Jesus, who is yet living among us … A man of tall stature, and comely, with a very reverent countenance, such as the beholders may both love and fear; his hair fair and tending toward chestnut, full ripe, straight to His ears, whence downwards more curling and wavering about His shoulders. It is parted in the middle of His head after the manner of the Nazarenes. His forehead is straight and unfurled; His face without spot or wrinkle, beautified with a lovely red; His nose and mouth so formed as nothing can be reprehended; His beard thickish, in color like His hair, not very long, but forked; His look innocent and mature; His eyes grey, clear, and quick.

"In reproving hypocrisy He is terrible; in admonishing, courteous and fair spoken; pleasant in conversation, mixed with gravity. It cannot be remembered that any have seen Him laugh, but many have seen Him weep. In proportion of body, most excellent; His hands and arms delicate to behold. In speaking, very temperate, modest, and wise. A man, for His singular beauty, surpassing the children of men."

Chapter 6

Cleanliness and Good Hygiene

There is much talk of human dignity today; at the same time few seem to make the practical application to their own personal hygiene, which reflects our dignity and the respect we must have for ourselves.

In the past, a young man was taught not only the proper care to be given to the eyes, nose, ears, and mouth, but also the value of holding his head correctly, how to use a handkerchief, the importance of keeping his fingers away from his face and out of his ears. From the time he was young, he understood that chewing gum, sneezing loudly, making unseemly sounds or grimaces with the face are improper and a sign of a bad education. He had the good example of his father, uncles, teachers, and other responsible men to show him the virility and charm of the good manners of a Catholic gentleman.

These good customs developed naturally in Catholic society as signs of the respect that we owe ourselves and our neighbor. It would be advisable for both fathers and sons to discipline themselves by adhering to these simple guidelines that make life more pleasant for everyone.

A sign of the respect we owe ouselves

Hygiene and cleanliness are integral parts of civility. They are a form and sign of the respect and esteem we owe to our bodies, to ourselves, and to our neighbors with whom we share the pleasures and benefits of social life.

They also constitute a condition and necessity for the conservation of health. Further, the clean and tidy person is always appreciated for the way he looks. On the contrary, one who presents himself with visible signs of a lack of cleanliness is an object of repulsion. Involuntary ignorance can be pardoned;

no one, however, pardons dirtiness, the lack of cleanness. Not subjecting oneself to the laws of hygiene results from a lack of a sense of personal dignity. It harms one's own health, leads to an early old age, and imposes on others the irritation of a repugnant companion.

Prevents sicknesses and promotes sociability

Medical studies attest that the lack of hygiene is the most certain cause of numerous sicknesses and the normal route to acquire many bodily and spiritual vices.

Hygiene begins with the body; afterward, it is applied to clothing; and finally it encompasses external ways of living, at work as well as at leisure.

It hardly needs mentioning that the daily frequentation of lavatories in the home, school, or public places reveals whether a person is well-raised. The well-bred person utilizes them with the maximum cleanliness and decorum, leaves everything in order, and always washes his hands before leaving.

To breathe is to live. Breathing is synonymous with living. Bad breath or shortness of breath diminishes the vitality of the person, reducing both the quality and at times even quantity of life. The first moments of each day, after the morning prayer, should be consecrated to physical exercise and hygiene. Such a regime gives a person a sense of well-being and good health. Taking deep breaths awakens the body, stimulates the organs, eliminates toxins, and prepares the ground for the intellectual and moral cultivation of the day.

The four daily baths

The four daily baths recommended by hygienists are
1. a mouthwash with a cup of water;
2. a bath or shower for the whole body;
3. the bath of fresh air;
4. a bath of sunlight.

Hands should always be washed before every meal. The fingernails should be buffeted and clean.

The importance of clean nails must be emphasized for Americans, who need to do – or love to do – all kinds of practical work that results in dirty nails. One of the first things your company notices is your dirty nails. After the face, the hands are what show and reveal the most about your personal hygiene. So, in order to show respect for yourself and maintain the respect of your relatives and friends, never forget to examine your nails and clean them whenever necessary.

To avoid soiling your hands and nails, today there are many different types of rubber, plastic, and vinyl disposable gloves, very inexpensive, that may save a lot of time in cleaning your nails.

The head

The head should ordinarily be held in a normal position, that is, erect, slightly inclined forward, without stiffness or flaccidity. One should avoid resting the head on the shoulders or chest, nor should one make any precipitous or jerky movements of rotation.

Affirmative or negative responses are expressed by the words "Yes" or "No," and not with a movement of the head.

A man with a hat should lift it slightly as a sign of respect before superiors, ladies, and sacred buildings, and statues.

Men should uncover their heads when entering a house, church, restaurant, club, or any other edifice. Women may keep their heads covered in company, inside buildings, during visits to hospitals and museums; in churches it is always required.

It is considered a sign of incivility to pass one's hand frequently through the hair, to scratch the ears or nose, to comb the hair, or twist a strand of hair in one's fingers. This behavior is discourteous, vulgar, and offensive.

The hair

The hair should be trimmed every five or six weeks. When cut, it gives the man a vigorous and forceful air; it is the style of the ancient Romans.

With regard to Western customs, long hair is a sign of disorder or ridiculous vanity. It often is the sign of a soft, effeminate character, a man inclined to vanity who spends long amounts of time on the hair, applying ointments, tonics, mousses or other products.

Dandruff should be treated with frequent washing and special shampoos and by keeping the hair short.

The face

The face calls for the greatest cleanliness. It should be washed with soap and water not only upon arising, but also during the day each time it becomes necessary and after any physical exertion that raises abundant sweat. Dry it with a clean towel.

Avoid passing the hands on the face or chin, or drumming your fingers on the chin or cheeks.

It is very annoying to see a person who is constantly moving his lips or running his tongue over them. Every movement of the lips that is not necessary for good pronunciation is uncivil and vulgar.

Every face is worthy of respect because it reflects the soul of the man. To give slaps, cuffs, strikes, or blows to the face of anyone is the supreme injury, because it indicates a supreme lack of respect for the offended party.

The ears demand rigorous cleanliness

The ears, like the eyes, are precious organs for our external relations. They merit very special and delicate care. They should be appropriately cleaned daily. This will maintain and preserve your hearing system by avoiding the accumulation of earwax, which often decreases hearing capacity.

The nose

This organ should be treated with special care. Everyone knows that it can be a focus of infection and hazardous germs if it is not kept clean and given the treatment demanded by good hygiene and customs.

It is repugnant and intolerable to see a person, child, or adult put his fingers in his nose. In addition to being repugnant, it is dangerous because it can cause an irritation that can become infected.

One of the acts that every well-bred man should execute with attention is the discreet use of the handkerchief to clean the nose. There are, however, few who do so with civility.

First, one should carry and use a clean handkerchief, which implies changing the handkerchief frequently;

Second, one should turn aside from the persons with whom he is speaking;

Third, he should be as discreet as possible regarding sounds, avoid making loud or rude noises;

Fourth, the handkerchief should be of an appropriate size, so it does not unfold like a banner;

Fifth, he should never look at the nasal mucus;

Sixth, he should fold the handkerchief as it was before using it, and return it to his pocket;

Seventh, he should not hold the handkerchief in his hand during a conversion, or leave it on a piece of furniture.

When one appears at a public function or solemn occasion in a representative role, as president, secretary or a speaker, the handkerchief may also be used for wiping the sweat from the face or hands, to cover a sneeze, or to clean the lips after drinking water.

Sneezing is an involuntary reflex action. Almost anything that irritates the nose can trigger a sneezing fit, including dust, strong smells, temperature changes, and allergies.

Only crude or rustic persons consider it impressive to sneeze with a great clamor, thinking they are showing the strength of their lungs with the inopportune noise. The sneeze spreads germs. Therefore, as much as possible, one should sneeze into his handkerchief; if the sneeze is unexpected, the hand at least should cover the mouth.

It is a good custom for bystanders to say "God bless you" when a person sneezes. The person should respond, "Thank you."

Contorting the face and making grimaces is inconvenient, not only in public but everywhere. It is also extremely impolite to purposely sniffle, snort, belch, or make any other vulgar sounds.

The mouth

The mouth is the preferred way for bacteria and germs to enter the body, above all, between the teeth. From this comes the need to keep the mouth very clean.

It should be washed morning and night, and the teeth brushed daily. After a strong meal, it is advisable to cleanse the mouth with water, as much for hygienic reasons as for civility. Frequently ulcers and cancer of the stomach result from the bad state of the mouth and teeth. Also, after eating some foods, such as those with onions and garlic, the breath can be acrid and make a person undesirable company.

A well-bred man never sticks his fingers in his mouth; he does not absently chew on paper or the end of a pencil; nor does he chew gum, chewing endlessly for no reason like a cow chewing its cud. Such habits indicate a lack of vigilance over self, a relaxing of civility, or ignorance of good manners.

One might recall this maxim: By his mouth the fish is caught and dies; by his mouth a man ruins his health.

Respecting ourselves and others

We should respect our own face and also the face of our neighbors. Any slap on the face of another is always a grave injury.

When he was a child, St. Marcellin Champagnat saw a somewhat nervous professor cuff the face of a student for his lack of attention. The good sense of the child, who would later be the founder of a teaching order called the Marist Brothers, reproved that brutal act and won from his parents permission to no longer assist at the classes of that master.

History reproves the action of the Jews who commanded the buffeting of the great Apostle St. Paul under the false pretext of having spoken too freely to a priest of the Old Mosaic Law. In the Mosaic Law, an unjust blow to the body of an adversary was fined with a single shekel, or $10 of our money. But a blow to the face was punished with a fine of 300 *denarii*, or $4,000. Other bad treatment to the head, such as to pull the hair, ears, etc. received similar penalties, and with just cause.

We should make it a custom to consider our neighbor as a member of the mystical body of Our Lord Jesus Christ and respect him as a creature made in the image of God.

Chapter 7

The Smile – The Laugh – The Grimace

The annoying habit to laugh without reason belongs to the fool, not to the civil man. Unfortunately, a certain school of behavior that burgeoned in the early Hollywood era considers it advisable to laugh at everything. It is the same optimistic school that teaches that constant joking and large toothy artificial smiles are always suitable. Everything is jolly and funny, an attitude that does not fit reality and is at variance with the life and thinking of a serious Catholic youth.

The man of past eras took care to compose himself either in private, because he was before God and His Angels, or in public, where he gave an example in society of how a Catholic should behave. For these reasons, his laugh was composed, his smile sincere and amiable, his demeanor serious but not forbidding. The American cult to spontaneity and optimism has done a lot of damage to this composure. This chapter invites us to think seriously about taking the correct attitude.

The smile

The animal does not laugh; nor does it know why it has pleasure or why it suffers. The laugh and smile are specific to man, a rational creature. No animal is gifted with this faculty of expressing its pleasure or sorrow by altering the lines of the physiognomy, because no animal has a physiognomy or is capable of thinking. Laughter and the smile are the external expressions of a mental process in man, which provokes in us a sentiment of admiration, surprise, or sympathy.

The smile is the complement and the perfume of our relations. It awakens sympathy, completes a gesture, enfolds the features in captivating grace; it is a reflection of a man's internal peace. The smile softens a refusal, attenuates the harshness of a remark, eases the severity of a contradiction.

To smile is not only just the physical action of an upward movement of the mouth. To smile is to effuse the physiognomy with an amiable, temperate happiness that illuminates and transfigures, causing the gaze and features to shine with goodness and goodwill.

The smile, mirror of our interior state, is as varied as the sentiments that animate us. It is pretentious when it expresses a sentiment of pride. It is ironical in audacious and combative spirits. It is admiring in one who finds himself in the presence of beauty, goodness, and truth. It is confused in bewildered and befuddled souls. It is amorous in compassionate and tender souls.

The smile is the flower of affability that has an affect on all our actions toward our neighbor: the greeting and farewell, the reproof and the approval, and so on. If charity is a rose, the smile is its perfume. The smile is the weapon that wins the amity of our neighbor.

Laughter

Laughter is the sudden joyful expression of surprise caused by some external action or fact. Within the limits of convenience and moderation, laughter is permitted in society. It is communicative, like sadness and tears.

When it is a natural manifestation of sentiments of happiness, the laugh should conform to certain points:

• It should not burst forth raucously or immeasurably;

• It should not make the voice crack or echo with noisy sonority, such as guffaws or horselaughs;

• The body should not contort or shake, as if attacked by violent stomach pains.

Only a fool laughs without reason

Immoderate or constant laughter reveals a person who is unreflective and superficial. In effect, the laugh is a balanced reaction to a contrast appearing suddenly between two objects, a disharmony, a disproportion between cause and effect, the means and end, the effort and result, etc. Laughter is, therefore, a genuine response to an unexpected or unforeseeable contrast.

Not everyone knows how to laugh. A cultured man knows how to laugh calmly; the fool laughs raucously. We find in the *Book of Wisdom* the following sentence: The fool raises his voice when he laughs.

Laughter is inconvenient when it manifests itself in the presence of dishonest or deceitful acts, a licentious word, a dubious pun or turn of phrase, or a censurable gesture. A person of good education does not give his approval by laughter or a smile to that which is contrary to good customs or morals. On the contrary, he veils his face with a look of disapproval or repulsion, and retires from the company.

No one should laugh at the defects of others, be they physical or moral, nor should one contrive traps to make the ingenuous and simple the subject of laughter. It would be very censurable for a child to make fun of the deformities of a person, or to ridicule a retarded person or a man with disabilities.

Forced laughter, that is, laughing without sufficient motive, is proper to fools and buffoons. There is also yellow laughter, the reluctant laugh that pretends enjoyment when one is really displeased. Such laughter is insincere and should also be avoided.

The grimace

The grimace is an exterior deformation and movement of the features of the face. When some persons sing or discuss with vehemence, they make unconscious grimaces, wrinkling the forehead, goggling the eyes, contorting the nose, the mouth, and the face muscles as if they felt a violent pain. When they write, some scholars place the tip of the tongue outside the mouth and squint one eye. Certain grimaces express mockery, others signify scorn, yet others, stupefaction.

Some persons are accustomed to accompany everything they say or do with some kind of grimace of the features. Even worse, they imitate and ridicule other persons, exaggerating their characteristics or peculiarities. All this should be rigorously avoided.

The caricature is the sketched grimace. It consists of representing in cartoon fashion the salient defects or abnormalities of the features of a person, while conserving fundamental features so that the sketch is recognizable.

When referring to imaginary personages, the caricature is a comic art that ridicules defects and vices. However, when it reproduces the essential and deformed features of a known person, it constitutes a grave fault against charity, because it invites the mockery and ridicule of one's neighbor, and robs him of the good name to which every man has the right.

It is not proper or comical to sketch caricatures of teachers or classmates in order to amuse friends.

A serene face represents a noble soul

One who has a natural, refined smile has at his disposition a powerful arm for the good. The smile of the virtuous man conquers others for the good, just as the sarcastic smile of the impious man can harm others.

St. John Bosco is presented as the most amiable of men, his smile and open gaze capable of attracting and influencing both the young and old. But there is no trace of intemperance in that smile. It is impossible to imagine this man, whose every act was turned to moving his neighbor to the love of God, bursting out in strident, raucous laughter.

St. Therese of Lisieux passed through this exile strewing her sweet smiles everywhere. She smiled to those who desired good for her and to the indifferent. She smiled because in all persons she saw Jesus, to whom she smiled continually.

Chapter 8

The Art of Governing the Hands and Feet

It is very important that a man should realize how the movements of his hands and feet reflect his feeling and thinking. Instead of following time-honored norms of behavior, today's youth is encouraged to make demonstrations of spontaneous feelings.

Instead of a greeting proportional to a person's degree of proximity or friendship, nowadays we see an empty, egalitarian handshake given to everyone everywhere. The hug that used to be reserved for family and close friends has become an empty universal sign. It has even become common to see young men hugging young women who are only casual school friends, or office colleagues giving each other hugs with a liberty that, to say the least, does not invite to virtue. This breaks the natural, healthy reserve that should exist between the sexes.

Our behavior of the hands and feet also leaves much room for improvement. We often ignore the good customs of Catholic society, which advise that different persons should be treated in different ways. Do you want to be truly counter-revolutionary and build a Catholic civilization? Learn how to govern your hands and feet while in the company of others.

Our gestures reflect our state of souls

The relationship that exists between the physical and the moral in man is so strict and so deep that the sentiments and even the thinking of a man are usually translated exteriorly by movements, gestures, and actions, be it voluntarily or involuntarily.

This is one reason we should learn to dominate our sentiments, subjecting them to a rule of behavior that is attentive to the persons with whom we deal. Likewise, we should be vigilant over our thoughts and repress every impulse of disorder and intemperance.

The gestures and actions that are the natural expression of the interior peace and serenity of our soul disappear rapidly when the winds of passion invade and perturb our spirit. Our gestures and movements then reveal disquiet, agitation, or contrariety.

To avoid these rough sentiments from revealing themselves in our social relationships, we should develop the art of governing ourselves.

Rather than just appear to be good, it is better to really be good. Certainly, if you are dealing with a person who is well-bred, he will discern your dissimulation. To pretend to be what you are not is a supreme fatuity. In order to present yourself as a good man, nothing is better than to be good.

Since a man's gestures and actions suggest his thinking, the best way to have polite and elegant gestures is to have noble and elevated thoughts.

The most efficacious way to develop actions that have dignity and beauty in a child or adolescent is to put him in contact only with what is good, just, dignified, pure, beautiful, and elevated. It is the same tactic used by master artists to educate students. For example, a music teacher cultivates and purifies the taste of his pupil by allowing him to hear only select pieces of good taste, executed by finely tuned instruments.

Sentiments translate into gestures

The great influence that the exterior habits of the body has on the state of the soul obliges us to exercise great vigilance over our gestures in our social relations. With regard to how we place our arms, let us observe the following rules:

- Avoid raising the arms over the head, making circles in the air or any such thing;

- Avoid crossing them behind the neck or on top of the head or behind the shoulders;
- Do not elbow your way through a crowd.

Various regular positions are:
- Both arms hanging naturally, without rigidity;
- One hanging and the other half bent;
- One on top of the other about the height of the waist;
- Arms crossed at chest height

No one, above all in company, should yawn loudly, accompanying this act with a ridiculous extension of the arms and spasmodic contortions of the body.

In normal conversations, words do not need the support of grand gestures. This same rule should be strictly observed when directing oneself to a superior. Large gestures of the arms and hands, as props for our thinking, are normally admitted in public speeches. In private discussions, simple hand gestures are sufficient.

The hands reflect a man's good customs

Hands should be washed not just upon rising, but also before meals and each time they touch something crass or dirty, or even simply suspicious. They should be dried with the towel destined for this service. Children, the ill-bred, and hillbillies easily violate this rule.

In company, it is not permitted to noisily rub the hands together, be it as a sign of satisfaction or to warm them.

Some ill-mannered persons use their hands too much: they take hold of the clothing or arm of the person they are speaking to; they tug at the curtains in the living room; they tap on the table; they finger objects within their reach; they pick off flowers in the garden or a vase; they point from a distance at other persons. These are not the ways of a cultured man.

Hand play, that is, playing with this or that person, trying to catch or touch one another, should be avoided rigorously. It is a sign of excessive familiarity and generates disrespect for the person of the neighbor; it can also awaken sensuality and the lower passions.

Only someone who is poorly raised takes the liberty of cracking his fingers or putting them in the mouth, ears, or nostrils.

It would be unpardonable, being in company, to scratch the head, the neck, the chest, the legs or any other part of the body. Anyone who would witness this would imagine that the scratcher has fleas or lice, or some skin or scalp disease. Anyone who lives cleanly and wears fresh clothing does not need to scratch himself.

That fingernails should be clean is primary. They should be neither very short nor very long. Also, they should never be clipped in the company of others. Employers of good sense do not have confidence in business applicants with long nails. Not only do they look like the talons of fighting roosters, they are also a sign of great vanity, pretension, and foolishness.

Let fathers and teachers curb the bad habit that some boys have of biting their nails. In addition to being foul and vulgar, it is very bad for the health. Who knows what dirt and germs have collected under the nails? Certainly such filth should not go into the mouth or be ingested.

The handshake

The handshake makes up part of the greeting, and as such is a complement to the personality. One should extend his hand only to persons he knows, to persons being presented by a friend, or to someone to whom he wants to give a spontaneous proof of confidence.

In the greeting of ladies, the man does not take the initiative in this gesture. The lady is the one who makes the first gesture of offering her hand, and the man should respond, because on the part of a lady this gesture is an indication of confidence. For the same reason, the hand is not extended to a superior: the superior is the one who first presents his hand, and in fact should do so.

In our Western culture, the man extends the right hand. If it is occupied, the objects should be passed to the other hand. In an exceptional case, the left hand can be presented, with a few words asking pardon for the irregularity.

One should offer the entire hand in its full length and not just several fingers, which would be quite impertinent. The open hand should be offered in a firm, straightforward manner; the hand should not be hard and tense. It would be bad taste and overly delicate for a man to just lightly touch the hand offered him.

One should not try to retain the hand of the person with whom one is speaking; if it is the hand of a lady, to keep hold of it would be an unpardonable lack of courtesy.

Offering one's hand to superiors should be made naturally and with simplicity, with a slight inclination of the head, the legs and heels together, the left arm held in a natural position.

The need for shoes and socks

Civility prescribes certain rules regarding the legs and feet, which were dealt with in a preceding chapter.

To walk barefoot is not acceptable. It would be uncomfortable in cold climates. In warm climates the feet will come into contact with all the dirt and vermin that proliferate in the ground. In humid climates it can even be the cause for catching colds or more grave sicknesses.

A man has need of shoes just as he does of clothing; in this he differs from the animal. Socks should also be worn with shoes. The abundant sweating of the feet is absorbed by the cotton or silk material of the socks, which have this important hygienic function. Therefore, in the name of hygiene and good social behavior, a man should wear the shoes and socks appropriate to the place and his social condition.

Shoes should be carefully preserved. Good care will increase the life of dress shoes. In the city and in general society, shoes should be polished and have a good luster; in the countryside there is no such need. A man dressed elegantly who lacks a well-shined shoe is like a salon with luxurious walls and a dirty floor.

Shoes should fit the occasion and occupation

There is a revolutionary custom being adopted today, even in good social milieus, of wearing sports or beach shoes at home, at school, and in other public places. Everywhere today we see persons of all ages – even older men – wearing thongs and tennis shoes as part of their everyday dress. They do not seem to realize how unseemly this appears. It also sets a very bad example for the youth, who are given the idea that relaxation and comfort is the supreme rule of society.

We have compassion on poor persons obliged to go barefoot; they not only are exposed to many physical accidents, but also they unfortunately find themselves lowered to imitate animals that were created to walk on feet without shoes.

Chapter 9

The Voice – Speaking and Conversing

One of the great modern myths regarding conversation is that we are entitled to "speak our mind," that is, to express our hidden thoughts or say whatever comes into the head at the moment. This is simply wrong. Such a way of acting was always condemned as inappropriate in countries under the good influence of Catholic Civilization.

Do not just speak, but think before you speak: that is the *first* general rule. A gentleman or lady never uses words to harm or demean another person. Being kind and courteous is more important than being considered quick and clever.

Second, we should be conscious of how we speak: the tone of voice and attitude it projects, correct diction and grammar, and so on. Parents and educators should correct a young man with a whining voice or soft feminine tonus. Let the voice, like a man's stance and actions, reflect a strong, firm manly nature.

Our voice transmits our thinking

There is nothing more beautiful than the human voice. The word being the principal means that we possess to express our thought and to communicate with our neighbors, it is invested with qualities most useful to know.

The voice fulfils a very difficult and at the same time marvelous role in our relations with others: it transmits our thinking and manifests the private workings of our conscience, to the degree we desire.

Truly, there is nothing as hidden, impenetrable, and inviolable as a human thought. Even if the brain of a great thinker could be split open or his cranium become transparent like the purest crystal, we could not discover a single thought in it.

With all the modern means of communication today, we can know what is happening in every corner of the world; however we do not know what the man sitting next to us is thinking unless he chooses to tell us. The same is true of the conscience – an inviolable private place with the key to open it in the hands of each man alone. This key is the word.

The power of the word

The word is the concrete expression of the invisible thought. It does not know the hindrance of borders or territorial limits. Customs workers can prevent the entrance of drugs and arms; but who can detain passage of the word? The word spoken by an apostle or an anarchist has the power to spread the seed of good or evil through entire regions. Since the word is one of the things to be most feared in this world, its usage should be regulated by strict laws.

The Book of Wisdom says that one who does not sin by the tongue is a perfect man. Sometime we hear persons who have spoken hastily or wrongly trying to excuse themselves: "It's nothing – just a word in the air, said without thinking." This is not true. Words are like money, and we all know that no one throws money in the air or out the window.

The tone of voice

In the whole human genre, there are not two voices with the exact same timbre and resonance. One man, for example, may have a rich, smooth voice with an elegant tone. He received from nature an inestimable gift, because a word of consolation offered by such a voice can give solace to an anguished soul. One should zealously conserve the treasure of such a voice.

If a boy has a voice that is too soft, he should practice exercises to make it stronger. Remember the great Greek orator Demosthenes who corrected his soft tone, strengthening his voice by speaking on the seashore over the roar of the waves

If the voice is hard or sharp, one should try to develop a more cordial tone by means of practice or voice lessons.

It is necessary to discipline the voice, to correct bad habits of pronunciation with the same rigor that one corrects poor posture. In elementary schools, teachers should instruct the children to pronounce words clearly and speak with composure, thus destroying early the defects and bad habits that could later become disagreeable in conversation or public speaking.

One should try to correct the defects of regional accents, especially hillbilly drawls or the slurring of words, and try to acquire in speaking the same discipline demanded in walking and acting: that is, we should have a clear, unaffected, and firm way of speaking.

We should try to eradicate from our voices what could cause our neighbor to make a lesser judgment about us: the dry or acrid tone, the impertinent inflections, the arrogant tenor, the irritating whine.

Tones to be corrected

The strident or impertinent voice pounds listeners, offending their sense of dignity and worth. It injures our relations with others, predisposing them to argument and discord. One should combat this acridity by trying to develop a tone that is smoother, more polished, deferential, and amiable.

These tones should also be avoided

- The biting tone that leaves behind hurt feelings;
- The tart tone that seems to want to quarrel;
- The ironic tone that humiliates our neighbor;
- The critical tone that attempts to show one's rare wisdom, but rather raises the antipathy and scorn of others;
- The affected, overly-refined tone, an expression of vanity;

- The soft languid tone of the lazy man, indicating a spirit without energy or a character lacking sound principles.

Conversation

One of the most pleasant ways to use words is the good, simple conversation. To converse is to exchange ideas, sentiments, and impressions between two or more persons. For man, to converse is a necessity – a greater or lesser need depending on his degree of culture and civilization – because it establishes between minds an elevated relationship that allows an exchange of ideas, teachings, convictions, and opinions about the truth, society, and practical matters.

But in conversation, as in business, there are thieves; these thieves are those who rob the conversation of its good fruits by using evil language. We should not lend our ears to them, and we should not allow our names to enter this infamous list of foul-mouthed persons. If all men would turn away from these indecorous people, there would be much less calumny, backbiting, and vicious gossip on this earth.

Good, cordial conversations often number among the most enjoyable and precious moments in the life of a man. When minds share the same desire of common good, to converse is to fraternize, to relieve one another from the heavy weights of life. It is also to instruct one another by sharing the cathedral of knowledge and rich experiences that each one can possess. A conversation can truly be a banquet of minds.

Good conversation in the bosom of the family is a certain sign of domestic happiness. On the contrary, where it does not exist, we can say that customs have fallen into decay and the family is heading toward ruin. In a house of well-bred persons, good conversation should turn around themes such as religion, art, culture, and general politics. Personal criticisms should be avoided at all costs, as well as business matters and prosaic concerns about one's health.

In a general conversation, all the family members should make an effort to deal with elevated subjects. Each one should try to speak in the right way at the right time, observing the essential rules of charity and benevolence. In this way we offer our neighbor some of our spirit of fraternity.

Rules of Conversation

Here are some rules of good conversation:

1. One should not say bad things about those who are present, and especially those who are absent. If someone ridicules another person, we should offer a calm and moderate defense or keep a profound silence that marks our disapproval.

2. One should not overtly praise the physical, intellectual or moral qualities of the persons present. Such eulogies lack delicacy, can embarrass the modesty of the person whose praises are being sung, and can plant a seed of antipathy and scorn in the listeners for the too-vocal admirer.

3. One should not make a criticism of a defect before knowing that no one in the company has the same defect.

4. It is bad taste to speak of one's own imperfections, because generally they appear without the need to be pointed out. Telling stories where "I" is at the center of the episode is not recommended among polite persons.

5. If one of those present makes an error in his presentation of facts, the listeners should maintain an impassive air, letting him finish his exposition. Afterward, however, one can speak and express his own differing opinion, entering into the matter with a delicacy of terms that does not speak of self-love or hurt the feelings of the other. The speaker who made the mistake, warned by such amenable words, normally does not become irritated by the correction or angry with the one making it.

6. Do not interrupt the one who is speaking or monopolize the conversation, rambling on about yourself, your family

or personal matters that are of no interest or perhaps even disagreeable to others. One should also remember the good advice of Lord Chesterfield: "When conversing, never take hold of a man's arm, hand, or jacket to oblige him to hear you. It is better to hold a man by your tongue than by his person."

7. One should listen attentively to the person speaking. If the conversation seems fastidious or prolix, he should not show or express his lack of interest or impatience.

8. If you are narrating an episode, avoid repetitious or useless details. Also avoid the constant use of certain words whose repetition makes the conversation bothersome or heavy for the listeners.

9. Do not enter into matters regarding private family affairs, or speak of your professional capability or the titles you have won. Wait until someone manifests the desire to know them. Then, respond with modesty and brevity.

10. Do not let the conversation fall into topics that your guests cannot understand or follow. An equally serious fault would be to whisper or speak in a low voice to someone in the company so that the others cannot hear what you are saying.

11. Avoid spattering the conversation with too many adjectives, reverberant adverbs, or banal phrases, such as, "It was a *very, very* nice day," "How perfectly wonderful!," "It was so obviously clear."

12. Avoid finishing your statements with the tactless: "do you understand?" Rather, if you truly have a question about whether you were well understood, you should ask: "Was I clear?" This avoids insinuating that your friend is not clever. It is a more modest approach that makes the blame of a possible lack of understanding fall upon you. Also, do not end or intersperse statements with inane and meaningless phrases such as "Right?" "You know?" "Got it?"

13. One should not alter his countenance or make theatrical displays when telling stories that can arouse extreme admiration, sorrow, or pleasure. The man who dominates his temperament does not exaggerate his expressions of joy or sadness.

14. Know how to conduct yourself if others express opinions different from your own. To end the exchange of ideas with neither a vanquisher nor a vanquished, it is necessary to close the discussion amiably, saying something pleasant, such as: "We may disagree on this topic, but that won't stop us from enjoying our fishing trip tomorrow."

15. Every fault against grammar is also a fault against good taste and good breeding. Therefore, use the proper case and agreement, avoid slang and solecisms, as well as foul or vulgar language. Also, do not replace "Yes" and "No" with "Yeah" or "Nope." Even worse is to answer "Huh?" in place of "What did you say?".

Chapter 10

Discretion in Words and Acts

The need for discretion in day-to-day life is especially important today when it has become a sign of the bold, successful man to speak his mind, or to discover and reveal the faults of others to get ahead in life. This is not only uncivil behavior, but it also is not a Catholic way to act.

Discretion is the tact and politeness that is learned at home from the earliest age. If a child hears his parents constantly backbiting and finding fault with others, even good friends and close relatives, he will learn to do the same. If he hears his mother or father discussing his shortcomings or faults with others, he will see no reason to be discreet about their defects or the private matters of the family. Indiscretion is a kind of vicious circle – one indiscreet act provokes and leads to another. Soon, the harmony and kindness of life – inside the family, the community, and society in general – is broken and destroyed.

The discreet man is master of himself, and admired by all. The indiscreet man follows his more base instincts, and is disdained by all. Let us know how to be discreet in our conversation.

Discretion is an element of charity

Discretion, the daughter of humility and prudence, is one of the most beautiful adornments of the virtue of charity.

It essentially consists in that elementary and indispensable honesty which moves a man to guard his tongue with regard to his neighbor's business. The discreet man will cover a defect or fault of another. When he can, he will cast a protecting shadow over the mistakes of others.

Discretion knows how to keep a secret; to cloak a confidential matter in a prudent silence; to close the ears to insidious conversations generated by personal enmities. In short, a man should exercise discretion in all the circumstances of daily life.

When reserve is necessary

At a private luncheon that took place some time ago in the Brazilian city of São Paulo, five bureaucrats and a General were present. Several years before, the General had been the leader of a political party that lost an important city election. The bureaucrats, intelligent, curious, and given to making intrigues, tried to steer the General to give his personal opinions about his colleagues in the election.

The General quickly realized their game. He paid sincere homage several times to the talent, abnegation and merit of the other leaders. He let all the responsibility for the defeat fall upon himself. He said nothing, implied nothing that could even slightly tarnish the names of the other politicians.

Here is a magnificent example of discretion. Certainly, the General could have been tempted to distribute the blame for his failure to win the election among the various party leaders. But he did not do so.

Now, some examples of persons who lack discretion:

- During a conversation, he divulges painful or embarrassing facts about others who are still living or whose memory is still present to those in the party;
- He reveals an event that the family or individual would like to keep quiet or is not yet ready to make public;
- He insists upon being introduced even when he is told that the master of the house is busy or is not in;
- He makes a visit or phone call during hours that are inopportune;
- He sneaks imprudent looks at the letters, packages, or private objects of other persons in their presence or absence.

More examples of indiscretion

If you are talking to a person and another person arrives who would also like to speak to him, it would be indiscreet not to cut your conversation short so that he can attend to the second person.

Discretion consists in respecting the time and liberty of action of your neighbor. It is indiscreet to take up the time of others with small talk and matters when this disturbs their work and ordinary occupations and activities.

It would be indiscreet and even impertinent for someone visiting the home of another to dispose himself freely – whether invited or not – to books, objects, and furniture, removing them from their ordinary places, to give orders to the maids, to change the family schedule to follow his convenience, in short, to arrogate to himself the title of independent lord of the house.

Private family matters are sacred

If hospitality is sacred, so also is what the guest saw, observed, noted, or came upon unexpectedly during his visit at a family home. There is almost nothing so odious in a man as to violate the secrets of a family in whose home he was welcomed and received good treatment. What can be more despicable than a person who, after enjoying hospitality and exhibiting mutual friendship and good faith, spreads to the four winds the less edifying things he saw in the home?

The person who consciously or unconsciously trumpets the private affairs of others is odious to God as well as men.

Whoever finds an object of value, a document, or a letter in a public place is obliged to return it to its owner, because the fact of discovery does not confer the right of property. Thus also, whoever by chance or artifice, comes upon some private matter of one's neighbor, does not have the right to divulge it. Revealing such defects or shortcomings would be an even graver fault if it would result in damaging a person's authority or dishonoring his good name.

Our neighbor has the right to his good name, his reputation. To detract from it is to commit an act of defamation, which etymologically means to attempt against someone's fame or reputation. It is a bad action before God and men.

The mischief caused by indiscreet words

A word of Eve in response to the serpent – when she should not have replied to him – was the cause of the ruin of all mankind.

The words of the daughters of Israel who praised David, preferring him to Saul, was the cause of a great revolution in that monarchy, forcing David to become a fugitive and be persecuted for many years.

The few angry words that escaped from Henry II, King of England, caused four of his vassals to impiously murder the Archbishop of Canterbury, St. Thomas Becket, inside his own church.

With a thoughtless word, a secret is divulged; by revealing that secret, a kingdom can be lost.

How many families could never wash away a stain in society caused by those few simple words – "Did you hear?"

Chapter 11

Good and Bad Curiosity

It may be surprising to some to find a manners book addressing curiosity. But anyone who knows human nature will understand its place in a manual for a Catholic gentleman. A man's curiosity – not a bad thing in itself – can lead to much wasted time and even a wasted life if he does not govern and direct it. Here we are reminded that in the end, each one will answer before God for time wasted in idle curiosity.

When curiosity is bad

Curiosity is the human tendency to know everything, good or bad, about a person or thing.

Curiosity is bad *first*, when it is indiscreet. We have already discussed discretion in the preceding chapter. Indiscretion, a fault that is committed above all with the eyes, can be likened to stealing the goods of others. It is indiscreet to read the letters of other persons without permission, to examine the contents of the drawers or closets of a person, to look at or read someone's papers or notes left on a desk or atop a work table.

It would also be indiscreet to listen to the phone conversations of others, or in our technical age, to open the e-mails or enter the private computer files of others. This would, of course, exclude the case of parents who must monitor the use of computers at home for the sake of the healthy spiritual formation of children and youth.

Curiosity is bad, *second*, when it is scandalous. It is scandalous when one looks at what is indecent, be it on the television, movie screen or theater stage, or in photographs, books, magazines, and so on. Today we must include at the top of that list the obscene pictures plenteously found on the Internet. Looking at such things is morally sinful.

Curiosity is bad, *third*, when it suggests purchasing pernicious books containing doctrine against the Faith and good customs. Love romances and frivolous novels are also dangerous traps by which the Devil snatches uprightness and purity of customs from souls, especially women.

Curiosity is bad, *fourth*, when it is idle. Idle curiosity consists in the blinding desire for novelties of all types: from political news to the latest scandals or romantic entanglements of neighbors or movie stars. It is idle because the person obsessed by such things looks at everything without seeing anything, without fixing his attention on immediate, proximate things. The only aim of this curiosity is to offer new information to others who have the same defect.

The conversation of the man with the latest gossip always starts with the eager question: "Did you hear the latest?" Then he pours his futile information into the ears of his companions.

When curiosity is good

Curiosity is good and praiseworthy, *first*, when it is natural, being a free, discreet expansion of the reasonable desire to know the persons and things that surround a man.

Second, when it is scientific, guided by prudence and Catholic teaching and animated by the noble penchant to penetrate the mysteries of beings and things, of studying the causes and laws that govern them with the aim of successfully interpreting the grand book of Nature.

A good and praiseworthy curiosity was found in these Catholic men who had a great curiosity to know more about their fields of study:

- Andre Ampère who made great contributions to mathematics and chemistry;
- Alessandro Volta, inventor of the voltaic battery;
- Louis Galvani, another great contributor to the science of current electricity;

- Louis Pasteur, famous for his breakthroughs in microbiology.

These and others were great learned men of science and, at the same time, men of faith. Clearly, scientific curiosity is a condition for discoveries.

Curiosity can occupy all your time

There are men who are curious to learn in order to acquire knowledge that enriches their minds and benefits society. There are others curious to know the habits and lives of their neighbors. The first quality is as praiseworthy as the second is detestable.

There are men and women who do not take part in the constructive conversation of a society. From behind a window or a curtain, they listen to private conversations, spying on the actions of others. They never miss a word, even the most indifferent, and are quick to interpret everything as they see fit. If they seek out or visit a person, it is not in order to give him pleasure or consolation. Rather, it is to find out what he is doing or see what new information he might provide.

A man with the vice of curiosity will enter the business place of another, conversing and speaking amiably with the secretary to see if he can glean some "inside" information. Should he visit the man's home, he does not hesitate to make friends with the maids or children of the house with the aim of hearing their gossip and small talk. Entering the hall and parlor, his eyes never rest. Nothing escapes them. If the lady of the house is writing at her desk, he stretches his neck to try to catch a glimpse of a few lines.

This idle curiosity is no less present in ladies. The curious woman never lets a strand of hair pass without examining it. That is to say, she is obsessed with knowing the words, actions, dress, and lifestyles of neighbors and acquaintances. As for the government and order of her own home, she pays little care to that. From the time she rises from her bed in the morning until the moment she retires, she is consumed with discovering new tidbits about this or that person, hearing the latest scandal, or discovering the latest new trend.

And domestic obligations? They are left aside because the ones who have this vice of curiosity will proclaim that such things are very insignificant, unworthy of their time or attention. In fact, they are wasting their time on trifles and ignoring their duties.

One day, when they stand before God, they will have to make a strict account for their time, and then they will understand – too late! – their grave error.

Chapter 12

Loyalty

This chapter reminds us of the importance of the spoken word, of fidelity to a higher cause, of the chivalric ideal of loyalty. It invites youth to put aside the theatrical and sentimental notions of the synthetic brand of loyalty that often comes from Hollywood, and adopt the true loyalty of the honorable man of Christendom. That is, to be a man whose word has meaning because he is willing to give his very life for the cause of God and fatherland.

Loyalty, a virtue of Chivalry

Honor and loyalty are almost synonymous terms that awaken visions of heroism and nobility, above all in youth.

The most perfect code of all the virtues is without doubt the Gospel. However, alongside it, institutions have been formed that present its principles, virtues, and magnanimity. Among such institutions the orders of Chivalry stand out in an eminent way. For centuries they have provided examples of rare and heroic virtues. Today there are still some remnants of these celebrated orders in the Orders of Malta, Calatrava and Alcântara, and the Order of Christ.

The fundamental precepts for the Military Orders included honor, loyalty, fidelity to one's word, sincerity of heart and death before ignominy. Unfortunately, however, almost everywhere the Chivalry inspired by Christendom for the protection of the weak and the oppressed, for combating the barbarian, egoism, and the lie, has been extinguished.

Modern day generations, ignorant of the magnificent facts of past centuries, look disdainfully at these institutions that in our times, under the winds of pride and sensuality, the direct fruit of Protestantism, have fallen into decay.

Today, loyal men of proven integrity are increasingly hard to find. With the increasing drift to paganism in the social institutions, the characters of men have lost their old temper, made of unbreakable honor. Hypocrisy, fraud, and the lie seem to have acquired citizenship in social institutions.

Movies constitute the modern school of the art of pretense; they are damaging the characters of many men and women, both old and young.

What is loyalty?

To be loyal is to be true to oneself and to one's neighbor. To be true to oneself, one should align his actions and words to his sentiments, and his sentiments to the laws of Morals and the common good. One is true to one's neighbor when he opportunely expresses what he feels and knows to be true, honest, and good, and not just what the other wants to hear.

Loyal persons, enemies of dissimulation, disguise, and pretense, are most rare. Loyalty is not only demanded in important and elevated matters. It is the foundation for relations between men in their daily affairs, as much for one who governs as one who teaches, for both the buyer and the seller, for the one who commands and the one who obeys. To be loyal is to respect one's given word, not to conceal a second intention, not to sacrifice the higher cause for the secondary. An honorable man has only one word, be it explicitly stated or manifested in another way.

Lies, disloyalty, and fraud create distrust and suspicion in our relations with others. In times past when good faith reigned among Catholic peoples, a hand shake sufficed to seal a contract. A piece of hair was sufficient surety of the inviolable promise.

The child is accustomed to say yes and no, in accordance with what he knows and thinks. But our current language is laden with dubious expressions, paraphrases, hidden meanings, reservations, and ambiguous terms. For the loyal man, his word is the mirror of his heart, the enemy of contradiction dubiety, and disguise. He speaks clearly, and says what he means.

A man without loyalty insinuates himself into the business of others, using his means or position to double-cross benevolent or weak friends. He freely promises without the intention to fulfill his word. He praises with his lips and reproves with the heart; he is red today and yellow tomorrow; today the rat, tomorrow the hawk. The loyal man does not assume two different attitudes: to be at the same time cobra and lizard, Pharisee and Publican, lamb and wolf, Catholic and free thinker.

Fortunate, indeed, is the man who could have this epitaph carved on his tombstone: "He was always loyal." It is, in effect, a synthesis of all the virtues and constitutes a grand eulogy. It proclaims the man who was upright, honorable, and faithful, a man with integrity of character.

Historic cases of loyalty

King Alphonse VII ordered his Castilian army to surround the city of Guimarães until King Afonso Henriques of Portugal would pay homage to him. However, Egaz Moniz, preceptor of the young prince Afonso Henriques, left the city with his family and offered their liberty and lives in exchange for lifting the siege. Touched by the loyalty of Moniz to his homeland, his captors spared his life and granted the request. King Afonso Henriques, the first King of Portugal, was thus saved from vassalage by the loyalty of Moniz.

William Marshal served King Richard faithfully as knight, vassal, ambassador, itinerant justice, counselor, and friend. On the King's untimely death in 1199, Marshall supported John as heir to the throne. Later, John falsely accused Marshall of being a traitor, confiscated his English and Welsh castles, and took his two older sons as hostages.

Despite this, William Marshal remained loyal to his feudal lord. He considered that breaking his feudal bond and oath would be treason and dishonor. On the death of John in 1216, William Marshal was chosen by his peers in England as regent for the 9-year-old Henry II and is ever known in England as the model knight.

When the King of France, John II (1319-1364), learned that one of his sons, held prisoner in London as surety, had fled the prison, the old King left his court and offered himself as prisoner in the place of his fugitive son. He spoke these noble words: "If loyalty and good faith were by chance banished from the rest of the earth, they would still be found in the heart of the King."

Biblical examples of loyalty

The classical model of loyalty in the Old Testament is the case of the sacrifice of Isaac by Abraham (Gen. 22). God tested Abraham's loyalty by asking him to take his only son to Mount Moriah and offer him as a sacrifice. Because of Abraham's willingness to offer even the life of his beloved son to demonstrate his trust and loyalty, God spared Isaac and blessed Abraham and his family.

The Second Book of Machabees offers another example of loyalty. Oppressed by pagan conquerors, the Jews were summoned to deny the truth of their religion by violating holy laws. One old man named Eleazar, although threatened with torture and death, refused to eat the pork that was forbidden by Jewish law. Some of the pagans, moved by pity, offered to bring him a different, acceptable meat so that he might give the impression that he was carrying out the King's orders.

He refused to do this and in a noble manner, worthy of his years, remained loyal to the holy laws given by God, saying, '*I will leave to the young a noble example of how to die willingly and generously for the revered and holy law*s' (2 Machabees 6: 28). After saying these words, he was dragged away to suffer torture and death.

These examples from Scriptures, like the lives of the martyrs, teach us the importance of being loyal first to the laws of God, even above the laws of country or family sentiments.

Chapter 13

Punctuality

Punctuality is a corollary of loyalty. In the preceding chapter, we noted that a loyal man was a man of his word. He does not say one thing and mean another. If he agrees to do something, he does it. This transmits to being punctual. A man who says he will be somewhere at a specific time, follows through on his word. To make someone wait, to disregard the time of others, is a lack of consideration for one's neighbor.

Parents play an important role in establishing punctuality as an important goal for their children. *First,* they give good example. *Second,* they help their children make schedules and follow carefully. Also they see that they are punctual in the commitments they make at home and with others.

Serious consequences

In social relations, punctuality is one of the most important obligations of civility and good customs. It is one of the essential elements of order. Without it, one cannot succeed in any undertaking.

We could refer to many cases where the lack of punctuality harmed important affairs, upset magnificent projects, unraveled the most convenient arrangements, destroyed powerful plans of action, or even changed the direction of political and national events.

Let us look at only two episodes from the battles of Napoleon.

On June 14, 1800 Bonaparte, taken by surprise at Marengo, fell back under the Austrians led by General Melas. But later, General Desaix arrived with his forces. The French were fast to bring up and deploy these fresh troops, and the Austrians were slow to mount their attack. The result was the grand victory of Marengo that sealed the success of Napoleon's Italian campaign of 1800. If General Desaix would have been late bringing fresh troops, the French would have lost. His habit of punctuality – he did not know that a surprise attack was planned – saved the French.

In June of 1815, Napoleon was in Waterloo waging an important battle against the English forces commanded by Wellington. Wellington was counting on a Prussian reinforcement to defeat Napoleon. Wellington had the advantage of a strategic position, but Napoleon quickly undermined his position. Everything relied on the arrival of the Prussians. On top of the hill at Waterloo, Wellington was keeping watch, counting the minutes that he could hold out.

When everything seemed lost, the Prussian army arrived, coming from behind Napoleon's troops. Caught between two fires, the French army fell into panic, fled the field, and Napoleon lost the battle. With this defeat, the Napoleonic dream collapsed. If General von Blücher, commander of the Prussians, would not have been punctual, the fate of Europe would have been different.

What lack of punctuality represents

Limiting ourselves to the general field of a good education, we can say that the lack of punctuality represents:

• A scorn for order and disdain for the rules that are the obvious expression of the will of God for us in our family and social lives.

• A disdain for the persons we deal with. When we oblige them to wait, their time is wasted and their affairs are disrupted because of our disregard. We can also cause them to become impatient.

• A contempt for ourselves, because one who commits to a certain time and thing should honor his promise.

From the social point of view, to make someone wait or not to carry out a promise in the pledged time is a lack of civility.

From a moral point of view, it can be an injustice, because our lateness can prevent others from fulfilling their duties. How often, because of a lack of punctuality, a person can lose not only an important contract or benefit, but also the esteem and goodwill of friends and business associates.

In the eyes of the well-bred Catholic man, everything in his daily life has an importance. The duty of punctuality applies to an invitation, a walk, a visit, or a family dinner just as it would to a critical political meeting, an important social engagement, or an action with serious consequences.

Both the one who invites and the one invited have the obligation to be punctual. If one is a superior or in a position of authority, a lack of punctuality is more than a breach of civility. His irresponsibility can cause serious consequences not just for himself, but for others. If one is an equal or an inferior, his lack of punctuality can be an act of injustice, stealing time from others, which can deprive them of some good.

The obligation to be punctual

St. Therese of Lisieux was grand in the practice of the "Little Way," which is to carry out every small duty well. She valued the virtue of punctuality so much that she said: "We should be so mortified that, when we are called, we should stop what we are doing immediately and answer the call."

Youths should accustom themselves to follow a schedule and be punctual in everything: rising, working, eating, resting, and praying. Not only does following a routine give the good fruit of peace and prosperity, it also teaches courteous behavior toward all – superiors, friends, and inferiors.

The Spanish have a saying, I go slowly because I am in a hurry [*Despacio voy, porque de prisa estoy*]. The person who is often tardy should reflect on this maxim. Proceeding methodically often gets better and faster results than rushing. The person who is always in a hurry is usually the one who is always late.

Punctuality
by Louis Carroll

Man naturally loves delay,
And to procrastinate;
Business put off from day to day
Is always done too late.

Let every hour be in its place
Firm fixed, nor loosely shift,
And well enjoy the vacant space,
As though a birthday gift.

And when the hour arrives, be there,
Where'er that "there" may be;
Uncleanly hands or ruffled hair
Let no one ever see.

If dinner at "half-past" be placed,
At "half-past" then be dressed.
If at a "quarter-past," make haste
To be down with the rest.

Better to be before your time,
Than e're to be behind;
To open the door while strikes the chime,
That shows a punctual mind.

Moral:
Let punctuality and care
Seize every flitting hour,
So shalt thou cull a floweret fair,
E'en from a fading flower.

Chapter 14

Amiability

It is easy to confuse amiability with softness, for example, to consider the smiling fellow who wants to be liked and avoids confrontations at all cost an amiable person. This is not, however, the amiability of the Catholic man. For him, the first rule of amiability is the willingness to sacrifice himself to please others in order to lead them on the path of Our Lord Jesus Christ.

The amiable man knows how to repress a sign of impatience. He never fails to correct, but knows how to do so with kindness. Instead of barking out commands, he adds a word of benevolence when giving orders. In preference to always imposing his tastes, he studies and tries to satisfy the likings of those with whom he lives. Such amiability is a sign of self-discipline and strength of spirit, not weakness. The truly amiable man will always be both respected and admired in the home and the workplace.

Forgetting oneself to please another

The virtue of amiability is most rare, because it demands apparently inglorious sacrifices and constantly puts brakes on our egoism. The best dictionaries either fail to define it adequately or give inadequate definitions. A common starting point for characterizing amiability is the desire to please. This definition, however, still needs to be developed.

To be amiable is to forget oneself with the aim of pleasing another. Even more: the amiable man will sacrifice himself in order to offer a legitimate satisfaction or pleasure to other members of society.

We can consider humanity as divided into two camps. *In the first* are those who struggle for their own interests, at times to the detriment of the good, interests, and satisfaction of others. *In the second* are those who defer their own personal comfort, even if it means some sacrifice on their part, for the greater good of their fellow men to lead them on the path of Our Lord. In this last group we find the Saints, benevolent souls who, following the precepts of God, seek the good of humanity in the spread of the Kingdom of Christ on earth, as well as apostles of Catholic charity under diverse forms.

Amiability is what conquers

The amiable man has the great joy of sacrificing himself for the love of God. Doing so, he lives not only for himself, but also in the hearts of his fellow men, by harmonizing his desires, concerns, will, sufferings and sacrifices with theirs. At the base of amiability is a certain sympathy, whose most excellent degree of expression is Catholic esteem.

How does the amiable Catholic man act?

He accedes in inoffensive matters, assists in arduous jobs – even the most common, eliminates obstacles whenever possible, facilitates the work at hand, excuses shortcomings and deceptions, and interprets in the best sense everything that comes from his neighbor.

He is deferential and accommodating toward older persons, bringing them the things they need or removing obstacles from their pathway. He is attentive and kind to ladies, foreseeing their needs and carrying out their small requests and errands. He is friendly toward his colleagues, showing them constant dedication, offering them support in moments of difficulty, encouraging them in adversities and relieving them in their task load in those times of need.

With inferiors, he attends to their just requests, listens to their complaints, examines their demands with interest, and gives them unequivocal proof of his dedication and esteem.

Amiability can be excessive and carried too far. One should not be self-deprecating, insist on services that others do not want, or take initiatives of command or superiority that pique or irritate others.

Timidity, or excessive shyness, can also wound Catholic amiability. For example, one should not refuse to contribute to the good success of an undertaking because of lack of confidence in his own ability or valor. Nor should someone refuse solicitations to read a poem or a story, play an instrument, or sing a song.

Some parents who ask their children to perform for guests make the mistake of excusing their children for being humble or shy if they refuse. Children should readily perform at the command of the parent, having the will to give them and others pleasure. Just as inopportune audacity is condemnable, no less is a systematic refusal to do simple things that would please others. In fact, such refusals generally come from pride or vanity.

An amiable King

A man who showed great amiability on a certain occasion was the King of Portugal John II (1455-1495). One day at the table he asked for a drink. An old knight, a veteran of his Africa campaigns, hastened to oblige him. It happened, however, that the glass escaped from his fingers at the very moment when he was presenting it to the Monarch.

The accident was greeted by laughter on the part of some at the table. The face of the old knight was blushing in humiliation when the King intervened, his gaze turned severely on the merrymakers.

"Why do you laugh?" he said. "Even if the glass fell now from the hand of this good knight, I can assure you that his lance did not fall in Africa!"

With this reproof, the ones laughing were reprimanded and the old knight consoled.

Chapter 15

The Braggart

He is called the "show-off" when he is small, the boy who loves to be the center of attention and give his childish opinion on all matters with great confidence and aplomb. Some parents make the grave mistake of considering such displays as charming or a symptom of geniality, not realizing they are helping to create that tiresome, unbearable adult called the braggart, who is described below.

The braggart fools no one but himself

Just as it is difficult to define the color of the chameleon, so also it is next to impossible to define the variability of the braggart who wants to shine in every topic and place. The term braggart designates one with a facility for words characterized by exuberance and volubility. Such exuberance generally comes from a high, egotistical opinion of oneself and little consideration for the thinking and convictions of others. His flow of words carries the braggart along, producing giddiness and self-delusions.

Certainly we are pleased to listen to an illustrious man speaking with understanding and discretion. On the contrary, we are disgruntled when we are obliged to bear the tiresome conversation of a braggart. Filled with a sense of his own imaginary importance, he touches lightly on all subjects and runs disparately over the most varied and unconnected themes, without a deep understanding of anything. In a short time we are tired of his loquacity and bored by his presumptuous air, and our only desire is to flee his company.

The braggart enjoys no credibility in what he says or proposes, unlike the truly intelligent man, who is modest and reserved. Quite the reverse, he dominates the conversation, not allowing others the time or opportunity to expose their own opinions, in this way depriving himself of the insights of others, and onlookers of the use of the word.

The braggart is not the high-spirited *bon vivant* that he imagines himself to be. The true conversationalist is lively and brilliant in his ideas, moderate in his opinions, reserved in speaking of himself, and discerning of situations. He takes into account the various circumstances, prudently judges persons and things, and expresses himself with goodness and tact.

In contrast, the braggart speaks in all directions at once, soon making contradictory statements. He violates the rules of logic in speech, plays with the truth, makes light of serious things, and ridicules acts of abnegation and sacrifice by his jocular tone and irreverent language. Through all his pores and from every word, egoism oozes from the braggart. He laughs at everything and dissolves the most serious topics – life and death, the sentiments of sorrow or pleasure, suffering and sacrifice – into vague notions.

The typical braggart has no authority on any topic, nor is he believed by anyone. Whether he realizes it or not, no one takes him seriously.

The Spanish have a proverb the braggart would do well to consider: "Tell me what you brag about, and I'll tell you what you lack" [*Dime de qué alardeas y te diré de qué careces*].

God chastises the braggart

In the time when the Philistines were hostile toward the Hebrews, a giant by the name of Goliath came out of the ranks and challenged the strongest Israelite warriors to single combat. Goliath laughed scornfully when a mere shepherd boy responded to the challenge. With a simple stone from his slingshot, David killed Goliath and then beheaded him with the giant's own sword. Thus God justly chastised the braggart.

When King Nabuchodonosor was considering the great improvements that his administration had given the nation and was thinking of imposing himself on the people as a divinity, he was struck with dementia, and for seven years he was confined to a house for madmen. Thus God resists and humbles the proud.

The pride of Diocletian, the ferocious author of the tenth persecution against the Christians, became so great that he had coins minted with this pretentious inscription: "*Nomini Christiano deleto!*" [I will wipe out the name of Christian.] He died in 313, the same year that the Edict of Milan was published by Constantine the Great, which gave peace and triumph to the Church. The name Christian was glorious, and the braggart Emperor lay forgotten in his tomb.

In a refinement of diabolical perversity, Julian the Apostate determined to find a contradiction in Jesus Christ. For this, he undertook the re-construction of the Temple of Jerusalem in order to defy those prophetic words of Our Lord regarding it: *There shall not be left a stone upon a stone, that shall not be thrown down.* To punish such a bold proposal, God sent forth fires and earthquakes that stopped the project from going forward.

Thus does God laugh at the proud men and braggarts who try to make war against Him.

Chapter 16

The Value of Distinction

Some modern men might argue that distinction is out of fashion. More and more of our politicians and leaders have jumped on the populist bandwagon, appearing in public in T-shirts and Bermuda shorts and drinking beverages straight from the bottle or can. They take on common mannerisms with the aim of attracting the people by "being one of them." They are wrong. Such vulgar attitudes may win the fleeting empathy of egalitarian spirits, but nowhere does it raise true esteem and admiration, born from respect. The real leaders are those who are models for the masses.

Today, more than ever, the man of distinction must be willing to follow principles, not the modern fashions. He should be strong enough to set a superior example and not follow the vulgar styles of the Revolution. He should cultivate from early years distinction in his bearing, speech, and thinking.

The various degrees of distinction

After the glory of God, the possession of means to assure a stable situation in life for themselves and their families is the general goal of almost all men. The next place should go to the pursuit of positions of distinction and honor.

Distinction is composed of moral values, noble ways of being and action that give a man a great prestige. Such distinction is so precious that many *nouveaux riches,* the overnight millionaires, would consent to give half their belongings in exchange for that distinction which they feel themselves to lack.

There is a high degree of distinction that few men possess. It consists of a harmonious conjunct of great capacities and rare, eminent moral qualities that permeate one personality and being. This assemblage of gifts projects itself on the physical exterior of the individual, illuminating his countenance, accompanying him like a halo, ennobling his features, directing his gestures, governing his whole person.

Below this high moral distinction there is a natural distinction that results from a harmonious proportion of body and physical characteristics, generally inherited by nature. Such would be the man of tall stature, erect body, raised head, proportioned shoulders, refined profile, fine hands, narrow neck, etc. However, from the point of view we are considering here, this kind of distinction is easily confused with elegance.

Clearly, no one chooses his body, picks out his natural capacities, or selects his aptitudes and first tendencies. We all receive the measure that Providence handed us to achieve our destinies. But a great possibility of perfecting oneself exists in each man. Just as good spiritual practices, diligence in work, and a constant elevation of ideas and sentiments develop our character, they also confer upon us a high moral and intellectual distinction.

In the same way, our external habits and customs will impress on our mien and our posture an unequivocal air of distinction or of vulgarity, proportional to the time and intensity of our noble or vulgar actions. Further, we know that we can correct, reform, or improve habits, adapting them to the laws of good taste and better social mores.

For this reason, we should work to improve our customs, deportment, and manners, and combat our more visible social defects.

For example, correct deportment gives an air of prestige and self-worth even to bodies less favored by nature with beautiful forms. Energetic action corrects laziness. A calm and self-possessed air reveals a man's peace and tranquility of soul on his physiognomy, and instills harmony and amiability onto the features.

Gestures also have a powerful influence, and when they correspond perfectly to what a man is thinking and saying, they increase twofold the strength and prestige of his words.

Facial expressions project a man's state of spirit

When governed, laughter and speech enhance the physiognomy; when ungoverned, they convulse the face, stealing all its polish and finesse.

One need only look at the faces of the Saints – the real faces, and not the sentimental caricatures that some religious books present – to see the distinction and nobility reflected in their features.

We recall here the story of that artist who sought many years for a model of great distinction and nobility of feature to sit for a painting of Jesus Christ in the Last Supper. Finally, he found a pious Roman monk. Some years later, after painting eleven of the Apostles who were present there with Christ, he sought a model for the last personage of the picture, Judas. After a long search, he finally discovered one man so vile and criminal of countenance that he seemed to express the traitor. The arrangements were made for the sittings.

One day, as the artist was painting, the man began to weep. When questioned about the reason for his tears, the man answered: "I am weeping because years ago, I was the one you chose as a model to paint Our Lord Jesus Christ in this same picture. Today, I pose for you as a model of Judas." He had apostatized from his religious vocation, turned to a criminal life, and his features and mien had degenerated to the point that he represented the opposite of that high moral perfection he had been called to achieve.

True distinction rises above human respect

Distinction is, therefore, a precious adornment of the personality, sought by the noble, esteemed among the poor, venerated by all as an incomparable jewel.

How to acquire such distinction – an effort which should begin in one's early years – can be summarized in these few words: to acquire good customs and to think on high things.

The man of distinction is never a slave to human respect. He fulfills his duties without the need to check what the people around him are thinking. He is not afraid to display his religious, political, or social convictions. He does not feel diminished by the poverty, rusticity, or ignorance of family members. He is not embarrassed of friendships or associations with the poor and ignorant.

The man of distinction does not boast about his awards; he does not take on ridiculous activities, like the marathon runners and sport maniacs who sacrifice their future and good for capricious, extravagant adventures.

The man of distinction does not boast about reading books by bad authors, or viewing racy movies or magazines. The man of distinction stays away from places that corrupt the intelligence and morals, and from secret societies whose programs are not openly known and discussed.

Examples of distinction

All the gifts of nature seemed to unite themselves in Pericles, a prominent and influential statesman, orator, and general of Athens in the city's Golden Age. In his youth, Pericles avoided public appearances, preferring to devote his time to study and the development of character. The first time that he spoke in public, he captivated all by his noble distinction of bearing and speech. Seeing such majestic and serene moral beauty, the Athenians compared him to a god. His eloquence, declared a poet, shone like a clarion and penetrated like a ray of light.

St. Vincent de Paul was the son of poor farm laborers of Gascony in southern France. He became the chaplain of the aristocratic Gondis family and the counselor of the Kings of

France, a man who universally incarnated the spirit of evangelical charity. When he heard his father had arrived in Paris, the holy founder of the Lazarists ordered the bells to be rung. He called the Priests of his Order to the chapter hall, where he introduced the simple peasant, saying, "Reverend Fathers, I have the great pleasure to present to you my father." It is a beautiful example of filial love and lack of human respect.

Marshall Louis-Hubert Lyautey, founder of the French Protectorate in Morocco in 1912, had no fear to openly display his Catholic convictions. On a certain occasion, he disembarked in Bordeaux on a Sunday morning. He was received with official honors, and the greeting commission presented him with a full program of festivities. There was no time, however, marked for Mass.

The Marshall pointed this out to the president of the commission with an amiable smile, saying, "But, honorable sir, something has been forgotten. Today is Sunday. At 8 o'clock I will assist at Mass, as I am accustomed to do in Morocco. I do not want to be less Catholic in France than I was in Morocco." And at 8 o'clock the Marshall entered the church to fulfill his Catholic duty.

Chapter 17

The Importance of the Greeting

The greeting is the external sign that gives a person our testimony of esteem, respect, or cordiality. It reveals and expresses our sentiments. To greet those we know is an obligation of charity. The way we greet a person reveals whether we are well-bred or untaught in manners.

The greeting makes the first impression, favorable or unfavorable, for persons who encounter us in our daily lives. From his childhood, a boy should become accustomed to properly greet the persons he meets. Not responding to a greeting or showing hesitation indicates that the individual still does not have the habit of courtesy.

In times past, extreme importance was given to the greeting, which was a public expression of the inequality of the social classes. A man learned the various ways to tip or raise his hat, the proper stance to take, when to shake hands and when not to, the bow and reverence for women.

The reverence, kissing the hand of a lady, is still used in ceremonials and formal gatherings, and every gentleman should know how to execute it.

Unfortunately, with the establishment of the egalitarian customs that have come to dominate today, most of the old uses of distinction have been abolished. For example, the man's hat, so expressive in the greeting, is gone today, and the distinguished rituals that developed around it also have gone by the wayside…

Four forms of greeting

Although the forms have been greatly simplified in our days, the greeting still has four degrees. *First,* there is the simple greeting or acknowledgement of a friend or acquaintance; *second,* the greeting with the handshake; *third,* a greeting with an embrace, and *fourth,* the blessing.

The simple greeting

We should accustom ourselves to greeting persons we know, especially our Catholic friends and superiors who deserve our consideration because of our shared ideals. It is an expression of our cohesion and unity in the battle against the vulgar customs of the modern day world.

Meeting a friend or acquaintance on the street or in a public place, the young man should look at the person with a pleasant expression and say, "Hello, Mr. Wilson," or "How do you do, Mrs. Martino." A child should never address an adult by his first name. Only a friend or close acquaintance should be greeted by the first name, "Hello, Mark," or "Hello, Louise." Avoid the simple "Hullo" and "Hi," or expressions such as "Hey," "Give me five," and other popular jargon.

Crossing the path of a person of authority or higher dignity, it is the younger or less important person who should offer the first greeting. "How do you do, Judge Richards." The superior replies cordially and briefly.

In the military world the same hierarchical principles rule. The person of lower rank makes the first salute to the officer of higher rank, who returns the salute. There was a notable exception to this rule in Catholic countries: the higher ranked officer saluted first when he met an inferior accompanied by his spouse; it was a beautiful sign of respect rendered to the sanctity of the conjugal union.

Greeting with a handshake

The second salutation encompasses the first and adds the handshake. Those who merit it are friends, relatives, and close relations.

The one who is more elevated in social position or older presents his hand in a spontaneous, cordial gesture, without pretension. The one who returns the gesture assumes the same attitude. The person of a lesser social position should not be the one to take the initiative in a handshake.

It is not necessary for a man to offer his hand to someone he does not know. However, after being presented or engaging in some conversation, it is convenient to give this proof of cordiality upon taking leave as a sign of amiability. It is rude to refuse a handshake, and such a violent act is justified only for very serious reasons.

During the handshake, the feet should be together and the body slightly inclined forward.

Greeting with an embrace

The third salutation adds a cordial embrace to the greeting. The rules that govern this salutation seem to have been thrown out the window today, with everyone – sometimes mere acquaintances – asking for or giving "hugs." Such general abuse, however, does not make such a practice advisable or licit. Rather, it robs the embrace of its legitimate meaning and worth.

The embrace, if it is to have some value, should only be given to relatives and close friends, among those whom exist a real harmony of views, interests, tendencies, and desires, great consideration and reciprocal abnegation, and values that realize the ideal of true friendship. The rules governing it derive, therefore, from the fundamental laws of charity, which make true friends participants in the same aims and ideals, the same sufferings and joys. These conditions restrict the embrace to the circle of true friends.

Nonetheless, as noted above, it is common today for these embraces to be given much more freely. There is no reason for these copious hugs distributed to acquaintances met on the street or in a store, or at the end of a shallow conversation filled with banalities. What value do these hundreds of embraces given profusely and almost flippantly have?

In the 17th century, Moliere was already expressing repulsion for such empty embraces unaccompanied by true sentiments. In his play *Misanthrope*, he censures the superficiality of such customs:

"No heart with the least self-respect cares for such a prostituted esteem.
> He will hardly relish it, even when openly expressed,
> When he finds that he shares it with the whole universe.
> Reverence must be based on esteem,
> And to esteem everyone is to esteem no one."
>
> *(Act I, Scene I)*

Therefore, we should exclude from our embraces all those who are not in the circle of our close relations. We should reserve a gesture so noble and significant only for those close to our heart, for our parents and relatives, for members of our household, for our benefactors and patrons, for persons of true intimacy, such as co-disciples, masters, our companions in battles and sacrifices.

Also, for those who are suffering, the victims of personal catastrophes, the poor who need an unequivocal sign of our understanding, it is licit to give an embrace that expresses our sympathy and offers moral comfort.

A Sacral Greeting: the Blessing

We have reached the fourth greeting, the most complex and sacral. This salutation completes the former with the request for a blessing, which invests it with a religious character. The blessing is in fact a prayer made by parents, to which God responds with His grace.

The venerable origin of this custom of receiving a paternal blessing goes back to Biblical times. Christianity, which restored and dignified the family corrupted by Paganism, also ennobled customs of respect and veneration that should govern relations in the familial society. The custom of the blessing deserves to be revived in our days, and would do much toward restoring the outward signs of respect children owe their parents.

The father is the indisputable head of the family, the king obeyed and respected in the home place. In a sound Catholic society, he is the representative of the wife and children before the civil powers, just as he is the representative of God before his family members. His authority is not received from any earthly power, because he is not the father by the will of the State or any positive law. His authority comes from God and, therefore, his blessing also comes from God.

For this reason, he blesses neither in the name of the law of the State nor in his own name, but rather, in the name of God from whom he received, through paternity, the investiture of supreme authority in the family. The mother, although submissive to her husband, shares this authority and may also give a blessing to the children.

The good child esteems and prizes the blessing of his parents. A greeting alone cannot satisfy filial love. At the first meeting of the day, before he leaves for school or work, as well as at the last adieu of the evening, the child approaches his parents, and asks the blessing: "Give me your blessing, my father."

The parent raises his right hand and makes a sign of the cross in the air in the direction of the child or over the child's forehead, saying the words, "I bless you in the name of the Father, and of the Son, and of the Holy Ghost," or simply, "God bless you, my son." If the parent gives the blessing from a short distance without touching the child's forehead, the child makes the Sign of the Cross, and kisses the parent's hand. The act has a profound symbolism, for God ratifies in Heaven what his representatives do on earth.

When far from the family, a son or daughter asks this blessing by letters and other means, and such blessings fall like dew on the soul of a child.

For similar reasons, it is also normal for a child to ask the blessing of his grandparents, godparents, uncles, and aunts. In Catholic countries, the blessing is not just something for children, but grown men and women are not ashamed to ask the blessing of their parents either privately or in public.

A head of a religious order or congregation also gives his blessing to its members. Also Catholic priests, our parents in the spiritual order, are invested with the prerogatives of paternity and give their priestly blessing.

The salutary Catholic custom of the blessing has unfortunately fallen into disuse. It should be restored, and the sooner the better. Happy the children of parents who greet them each morning with a blessing! And blessed the home where this sacral representation of paternal authority and filial submission finds daily expression.

Greetings in Church

The Church is the house of God and a place of prayer. For this reason, it is not the place for small talk, conversation, or laughter. In Church one does not greet his friends or acquaintances. In exceptional cases, acknowledgement of another can be given by a simple inclination of the head, but never with a handshake. Greetings and conversations should be reserved for after one leaves the Church.

When passing by a Church or Chapel that houses the Blessed Sacrament, Catholics should make a sign of respect to the Divine Presence. If a man is wearing a hat, he should remove it, or make a small bow or inclination. If he is not wearing a hat, he should make the Sign of the Cross. Similar signs of respect may be made when passing before holy images or family altars.

Greetings in the home

We should form the good habit of greeting the persons we live with, a custom that makes life more pleasant and sets a good example for everyone. A simple, "Good morning, my dear," from husband to wife, sets the tonus for the day.

We should also maintain the habit of rising to greet persons who have just entered the room. It is a time-honored display of respect to be shown to a person older or more important than you, someone you are meeting for the first time, or one traditionally shown special respect: a priest, official, or a prominent or distinguished person. It is not normal for the parents or older persons to stand to greet children or youth. Adults should only rise for others as a sign of high consideration. One does not rise for equals or inferiors except on very special occasions.

When a seated adult receives a friend of a young daughter or son, he cordially smiles and says some words of welcome. If the youth approaches the adult to greet him, the latter can extend his hand to be shaken.

Hosts and hostesses should rise and go to greet all arriving guests at social events, but once the party is underway, it is unnecessary to stand every time someone enters a room.

Standing and offering your seat to an elderly or infirm person or a fragile lady on a crowded subway or train is both courteous and an act of charity.

Examples from Scriptures

The Scriptures is a code of civility. Let us look at just a few examples. What a charming scene when the Angel Gabriel appears in the house of the Virgin, saluting her with the most beautiful of prayers: *Hail Mary. Blessed art thou among women.* And the Virgin, taken by surprise by such marvelous words, responds in her simplicity, *Behold the handmaid of the Lord…*

When Our Lady learned that Elizabeth was with child, she did not delay to make plans to travel from Nazareth to Hebron to congratulate her cousin for this high favor from God. At the meeting, the one who initiated the greeting was the Blessed Virgin, who was younger in age even though she was superior to Elizabeth in dignity: *And Mary entered into the house of Zachary and saluted Elizabeth. And it came to pass that when Elizabeth heard the salutation of Mary, the infant leaped in her womb. And Elizabeth was filled with the Holy Ghost.* (Lk 1:40-41)

Her words were accompanied by a prodigy of grace: the sanctification of John the Baptist, who leaped with joy in his mother's womb. It is to commemorate and imitate the humility of Mary in this greeting that the laws of certain religious congregations impose on the superiors the initiative of greeting.

Chapter 18

The Family Milieu

The tone of the Catholic family should be one of a natural and modest restraint. *First*, it is important to note that the Catholic home should not only be a serious place, but it also has something sacred in it, and as such it should be treated with respect. It is not a place for children to jump on the furniture, flop on the couch and chairs, or run around barefoot and half-dressed. The unfortunate modern tendency to idolize casual living and comfort has slowly undermined the seriousness and sound customs of the past that emphasized a serene orderliness, which instilled harmony and happiness in the home.

Second, this natural restraint should also be present in the relations among the family members, as it was in times past. In a family ambience marked by the spirit of Catholic affection, there is a profound natural respect of youth for their parents and elders. Young men are raised also with the notion that, as men, it is their obligation to protect and assist their mother and sisters. This respect for the dignity of others should manifest itself in all the familial relations.

This chapter is an invaluable call for Catholic parents and youth to re-think the American tendency to be casual, and begin to cultivate a ceremonial Catholic spirit in the home.

The family is the first school of civility

The family should be the first school of civility. Everything in it is sacred and therefore worthy of respect, not only the parents, representatives and depositaries of divine authority, but also the dwelling itself, the paternal home, the place where one lives and sleeps.

Since the home is the image and reflection of the family, it should be honored. Family members should guard its cleanliness and decorum, and everyone should live in it with dignity, discretion, and restraint. How blameworthy would be one who dishonors the family, or introduces discord, conflict, and deceit into it. By the manners and relations that reign between the parents and children, one can judge the degree of dignity and culture that exist in a family, just as one can know the virtues practiced in it.

Further, future citizens are formed in the image of the domestic virtues. The future of a nation depends, therefore, on the good constitution of the family, the first social cell, in which respect, reciprocal love, mutual abnegation, and charity should reign and flourish. These virtues radiate from this nucleus through the entire society. Strong families are the bastion that protects the happiness of the whole.

Honor thy parents

To love and respect one's parents is a divine precept: *Honor thy father and mother.* It would be callous, foolish, and unnatural for a child not to fulfill this duty toward those who, after God, give them all the goods that come to them. Who could calculate the total sum of the labors, sacrifices, and care that parents take upon themselves for their children? A son can never pay, so to speak, the debt of blood, sustenance, and education that he received from good parents. He will remain eternally a debtor to those who sacrificed for him.

Youth should pay no attention to certain revolutionary and anti-natural theories about the independence of children, in which the God-State replaces the parents. This nefarious doctrine breaks the natural bonds that bind family members together. These egalitarian teachings serve to dissolve homes, destroy the barriers of respect and love, and make a blessed sanctuary into a den of discord or a kind of inn whose inhabitants receive food and bed, but nothing more.

First, the father must acknowledge God as the origin of his authority, and then affirm such authority, or the children easily will become insubordinate and rise up against him. If he allows his children to impose their own wills on the household, they will lose respect for him. The children will become egoists, and the father will be humiliated, submitting to the demands and impertinences of the children. The mother will also suffer, bearing the ingratitude and capriciousness of those so dear to her. The balance of the family will become upset because paternal authority is lacking.

St. Francis de Sales noted that the affection borne by fathers to their children is not called friendship, because friendship supposes a certain equality in vocation, rank, or aims. Such equality, he continued, should not exist in the affection of fathers for their children. The love of fathers is, he says, a majestic love, and that of children a love of respect and submission. Everything in a Catholic society, the manner of being, the speech, the gestures, even the way of dressing, used to reflect this wise thinking.

For a son to be confident, calm, and secure, the father and mother must show a stable seriousness in the day-to-day relations with their children. If they are constantly playing, joking, and making life look like a game, they teach their children not only that life is not serious, but that authority is frivolous and clownish.

The well-bred young man

The manners of youth should be the same whether they are in the home or outside of it. Some young men make great efforts to appear amiable, respectful, and helpful outside the home, giving the impression of being fine, upstanding youth. When, however, they enter the family circle, they forget their principal duties. They abruptly change their way of being, taking on an acid, somber, and taciturn air. They are disagreeable, short in speech, disposed to quarrel. Their exterior is untidy, their dress disordered, and they fall into impolite silences. They act as if they were confined in a penitentiary, not enjoying the company of the family. This spirit destroys family life, turning what should be a small Eden for all into a kind of purgatory.

The well-bred young man, on the contrary, contributes to the happiness of the family circle by his very presence. He does his part to see that everything is velvet carpeted - in his way of being, gestures, words, expressions, and attitudes he assumes toward the other family members.

In the morning at first encounter, he greets his mother or father and receives their blessing. At night, upon retiring, he observes the same ceremonial. He does not absent himself from the home without previous warning or permission, in accordance with his age. He appears at the table at the proper hour, because being a member of the domestic society, he is obliged to observe the schedule established by the head of the family. He passes many hours of Sundays and holy days with his family, engaging in the good conversations that pertain to family matters or touch on business, politics, and civil life. By hearing the judgments of his elders about persons and things, he broadens his ideas, fortifies his own judgment, and, something that is very important, takes on the spirit of the family, which is a sacred legacy for a good son.

A well-bred young man often accompanies members of his family on outings and visits. He is the diligent and distinguished companion of his father. He is the protective support of his mothers and sisters, opening doors for them, drawing out their chairs at the table, careful in his words and actions not to offend their more delicate sensibilities. He tries to interest them with an amiable tone and conversation.

In the bosom of the family, he is quick to obey. He listens with respect and docility to the counsels of his parents, confiding in their experience. When it is appropriate, he shares his thoughts, hopes, and dreams of the future with his parents, and gratefully accepts the guidance they offer him.

How different is the behavior of the unnatural, disrespectful, and unloving child. We see him full of himself, infatuated with his personality, imagining himself superior to his parents in qualities or knowledge, speaking to them arrogantly, treating them with a certain air of scorn, disputing with them, denying their assertions, berating them at times for what he considers the manias of the older generation.

Such a son is unhappy and scorned by good men. Society should shun him. Certainly he is heading for great unhappiness in life.

Love and respect for siblings

Among the children of the same family, a mutual respect and sincere love should reign. Brothers and sisters should love one another since they share the same name, the same blood, the same traditions and virtues of their common patrimony.

The eldest should give good example and protection to the others. Boys owe their sisters a respectful, delicate love, by which they should avoid causing them annoyance and disgust. They should be their natural and vigilant protectors, rendering them services and convenient assistance, such as lightening their work, carrying their packages or heavy things, always ceding to them the better seat. It is in the practice of fraternal charity in the home that a boy learns the first and best lessons of civility.

Respect for elders

All these laws apply to the relations between grandsons and their grandparents. Their advanced age is all the more reason for virtuous and well-bred children to show them veneration and respect.

Parents should always be addressed by their proper titles: Father and Mother, or Papa and Mama, or similar terms of address. These words are sacred and signify both respect and affection. Children should never address their parents by their first names, or in vulgar or common terms, such as "old man" or "old woman."

The good son loves his parents not because of their fortune or social position, but because they are for him the representatives of God. For this reason, if they should fall into misfortune, he would redouble his affection and do everything he could to ease their burden in life. Acting in this way, he is certain that he will be worthy of the blessing of his progenitors. He realizes the truth of the words of Scripture: "He that honors his father shall enjoy a long life: and he that obeys the father, shall be a comfort to his mother."

The words of Holy Scriptures

Scriptures affirms the importance of honoring one's parents:

"For God has made the father honorable to the children: and seeking the judgment of the mothers, has confirmed it upon the children." (Eccles 3:3)

"Children, obey your parents in all things: for this is well pleasing to the Lord." (Col 3:20)

"A wise son makes a father joyful: but the foolish man despises his mother." (Prov 15:20)

"He that honors his mother is as one that lays up a treasure. He that honors his father shall have joy in his own children, and in the day of his prayer he shall be heard." (Eccles 3: 5-6)

"He that fears the Lord, honors his parents, and will serve them as his masters that brought him into the world." (Eccles 3:8)

"Honor thy father, in work and word, and all patience, that a blessing may come upon thee from him, and his blessing may remain in the latter end." (Eccles 3: 9-10)

General guidelines for the young man

The first proof of love for parents is to render them obedience and submission in everything, except what is not licit. A son should never answer his parents with "No!" or "I don't want to!"

In responding to parents, it is praiseworthy for youth to use the respectful "Yes, sir" or "No, Ma'am." This good practice should be adopted from early childhood. It establishes a tone of respect in the home and affirms the parents' authority.

Children should not be inopportune or demanding in their requests to their parents. It is even worse to show resentment should one receive a negative reply to some request.

Avoid bothering or interrupting your parents when they are busy. If you need to interrupt them, always do so politely, "Excuse me, Mother, I'm sorry to bother you, but I need ..." Do not contradict them or respond to their commands with dark looks or pouting expressions.

Do not speak of any family matters that can prejudice the honor of your parents or siblings. Do not broadcast their defects or criticize them to your friends. Instead, cover for them, excuse them, have compassion on them.

Avoid every expression of scorn or injury, as well as arrogant, resentful, or impertinent words. In the Old Testament, God fulminated with words of death the sons who curse or swear at their parents.

Do not make disrespectful gestures in front of them, such as shrugging the shoulders, turning the back on them, shaking one's head, stamping the feet, raising the voice, or what would be truly heinous, threatening or striking them.

Chapter 19

A Youth's Relations with His Superiors

This chapter sets out important principles of authority. When a parent sends a child to school, he is delegating his natural authority to the teacher. In effect, he tells his son, respect and obey your teacher as you would respect and obey me. In times past, when parents sent their son to a Catholic school, they could assume that their child would be formed according to sound principles and learn virtues as well as reading and math.

Since Vatican II, this is no longer the case. Often, the Catholic schools are breeding grounds for social activism. Instead of the Catholic Catechism, students have Comparative Religion classes to learn tolerance for all religions. The sex education classes also can be more explicit and vulgar than those in public schools.

It is important for parents to inspect not only the course material their children will study, but also to know about the morals and character of the teachers. Entrusting a child to the authority of a teacher sends the implicit message to the child that he can trust and admire that person. If the teacher's values and thinking are different from the parents, this can create conflict in the child and in the home. One can easily understand why so many Catholic parents today have resorted to home-schooling or alternative Catholic schools that use the Baltimore Catechism and demand a proper respect for authority. They rightly choose to affirm and strengthen their parental authority, instead of see it contradicted and weakened.

The teacher

Paternal power and their prerogatives are in part transferred to other persons: it is what constitutes the right of tutelage.

The tutor is, therefore, according to the etymology of the Latin word *tutela*, the guardian, the one who protects, the one charged by the parents to take care of their child. When a teacher is inspired by the principles of the Catholic faith and reason, the student should consider him a delegate of his parents, and therefore, a representative of God. For this reason, the student owes him respect, submission, and love, as to a second father.

The student should give teachers the demonstrations of respect that they deserve, greeting them when they meet them, removing their hats in their presence, standing when they enter the classroom, and always addressing them by their titles: Prof. Jones, Dr. Kingston, or Mr. Phillips. In responding to questions, one should answer clearly and distinctly, "Yes, sir" and "No, sir." The youth should have much confidence in his superiors, without an excessive familiarity.

Listen well to their corrections and when necessary, humbly receive the punishments they administer for your faults, without showing anger or resentment. At the end of the punishment, it is advisable to thank the superior. This act denotes honor and a sense of duty, since the student acknowledges that the teacher was making a correction of his defects for his own good.

When the student is questioned by a superior about the action of some colleague, he should respond with simplicity and frankness, principally if it is a matter of preventing or remedying some evil. Silence in such a case would harm the companion instead of help him. Let the youth give the requested information staying within the limits of the question and without elaboration, so that he does not fall into the bad habits of entering into intrigues and gossip.

Without being subservient, the young man should always be grateful to his superiors. Gratitude is a precious garment that makes a youth agreeable to all. Those who practice it attract to themselves the gifts of Providence. The noble young man can forget the benefits that another owes him, but he never forgets those he has received. He should avoid the company of those who speak against superiors. It is a sign of a bad character and a complete lack of gratitude.

When the educator is a priest or religious, he adds to his authority the fact of being a representative of the Church of Christ, which makes him an ambassador to the youth, according to the order received from the Divine Master, "Go and teach all nations."

Quintilian on the good student

Quintilian, the famous Roman teacher who opened a school of rhetoric in the 1st century gave this advice to students:

"Students should not love their masters less than their studies; they should consider their teachers as their spiritual parents.

"This pious conviction will assist their progress, because they will listen with docility, believe in the truths taught, and desire to become like their masters. Students should have a joyful and tranquil spirit. When they are corrected, they should not become angry. When praised, they should not become conceited or puffed up in order to conserve their zeal for study.

"Just as it is the duty of the master to teach, it is the duty of the students to show docility in learning. One thing without the other will not give a good result." (*De Institutione Or.* II, 2).

Religious superiors

At the apex of the religious hierarchy, we have the Supreme Pontiff, the Vicar of Jesus Christ, to whom all power on heaven and earth was given. Below him are Bishops and parish priests, the pastors of our souls. By the sacred character with which they are invested, they should be venerated, respected, and loved. An offense directed against them would be doubly grave. God chastises those who show contempt to his faithful ministers.

One should make the first greeting to every ecclesiastic you meet, even if you do not know him by name, because the greeting honors his character as priest and the religious habit that represents the Church of Jesus Christ. Every well-bred man will cede the right of way and best place to a priest as a sign of proper respect.

Greeting a Bishop, one should kiss his ring; in receiving his blessing he should drop on one knee before him, not just because of the grandeur of his episcopal character, but also because of the relic of the Holy Cross that Bishops usually wear inside their pectoral cross. Good Catholic youth should often ask the blessing of priests or Bishops.

When an ecclesiastic visits the family of a student, he should receive the place of honor and special attentions. The head of the house should pay this public tribute to the priest. No other guest, even a distinguished one, should be resentful of not having the place of honor at the table or in the living room.

Corresponding to the homage he receives, the priest should reflect in his person the dignity of his position, always displaying the style, tone, and expression worthy of a man consecrated to God. It hardly needs to be said that his morals and ethics should be impeccable to be worthy of the sacred trust placed in him.

Civil superiors

Another type of superior are representatives of the civil authority. From the President of the Nation to the Mayor of the city, all persons who exercise a parcel of public power are for this reason invested with dignity; because of their office, they merit a special respect and attention. Religion imposes on the Catholic the duty of obedience to constituted authorities, telling us that "all authority comes from God."

If the social organization gives a man advantages to progress in his material and spiritual life, it is only just that he should pay tribute to the representatives of the social order by offering them respect and gratitude for their public service.

The elderly

The elderly also deserve special treatment. The expression of such respect and esteem lies in small acts of kindness: standing aside to let an elderly man pass first, helping a lady down the steps or into the car, a friendly greeting accompanied by a few words. Youth should develop the good custom of visiting elderly family members and friends, not just when they are sick or in the hospital, but on a regular basis. Bringing them small gifts of fruit, flowers, or freshly baked food is a thoughtful gesture.

Need it be said that when parents or grandparents can no longer care for themselves, the Catholic child has the obligation to maintain them physically, morally, and psychologically, as well as to surround them with the proportionate degree of respect and affection they deserve. Doing this, the son is just returning the favors he received when he was a child.

Today we have the bad tendency to look down on the elderly and despise the things of the past. Our modern education overvalues the importance of youth and has an exaggerated idea of the need to be up-to-date. This adoration of youth and the latest fashion has reached such a point that the elderly see themselves set aside and even excluded from public deliberations, counsels, and meetings, where they are viewed as out-of-date.

Linked to this adoration of youth is a culture that teaches that the most important thing in life is to seek pleasure and have fun. This attitude breeds the habit of egoism. Instead of admiring the wisdom of the elderly, the fruit of discernment, long experience, and valorous self-sacrifice, nowadays the elderly are disdained.

Every sensible person with a medium level of civility recognizes the superficiality of a young man who brags incessantly of his own talents, flaunting progress and ridiculing the past as outdated, and who scorns the advice and stability of judgment of those with greater experience. Shallow youth like this avoid the company of the elderly, imagining that old people are fools, always repeating the same things, opposed to modern ideas and the joys and pleasures of youth.

Nevertheless, it will always be the sign of the well-bred man to show the elderly all respect and the most delicate attentions. He should show such esteem not only moved by charity for the infirmities that often accompany aging, but out of respect for the wisdom and merit of his worthy elders.

"Do unto others what you would have them do unto you," says the Gospel. Yes, treat the elderly with deference, sympathy, and veneration, so that after they have struggled and suffered, when they are in the somber, austere winter of life, they might have the consolation of enjoying contact with the younger generations.

Examples of respect for superiors

Young Samuel, a future judge of Israel, was resting one night before the tabernacle. Suddenly he heard a voice that called him, "Samuel! Samuel!" Thinking that it was the voice of the High Priest, he replied, "Here I am, master, for you have called me!"

But it was not the High Priest, it was the voice of God. This scene was repeated a second, and then third time, until Samuel realized that the call was from God and he responded, "Speak, Lord, for thy servant is listening!" It is a beautiful example of the respect and obedience owed to masters.

For eight years Alexander the Great received lessons from Aristotle, the greatest philosopher of Ancient Greece. This worthy master made a great effort to develop qualities and virtue in his student. Grateful for these wise teachings, the valiant conqueror of Asia was accustomed to say, "I owe more to Aristotle, my master, than to Philip, my father. The latter gave me life, but the former gave me the good life [of contemplation]."

Theodosius the Great, one of the most famous Roman Emperors, confided the education of his two children Arcadius and Honorius to a preceptor of great capacity and virtue named Arsenius. One day during the lesson, the Emperor entered the classroom. The master Arsenius was standing and the princes were seated. Theodosius was displeased with the lack of respect his sons were showing their master. He reproved them vigorously and demanded that the two boys stand while Arsenius, seated, gave the lesson.

"My sons," said Theodosius, "to your father you owe the life of your body and the hope of a crown. But to Arsenius, you are indebted for an even more precious good: a good education that will make you virtuous and worthy of the throne."

As punishment for the lack of respect shown on this occasion, the Emperor ordered his sons to pass eight days in court without wearing the insignias of their dignity.

Chapter 20

Traveling

As a young man matures, he will encounter occasions when he will be taking trips by bus, train, or plane. The manners of a well-bred youth are an integral part of him, and will be the same whether he is in his family automobile or on a trans-continental flight to France. One whose good manners are assumed only in company is a veneered Catholic gentleman, not a real one.

Dressing appropriately

It is quite agreeable to travel with courteous and civil companions. On trips one should dress with appropriate decorum, decency, and tidiness. It is a duty of charity not only toward the persons with whom you travel or encounter, but also a duty toward yourself because a man is judged by his clothing, especially on travels.

Not so long ago, this rule was generally followed. Airports, train terminals, and bus stations were peopled with men in suits and women in dignified travel attire. Today, the trend toward the casual and vulgar is dominating everywhere. Following the new criteria, decency and aesthetics are no longer important; the only thing that matters is to be comfortable. So, we see persons of all levels in society dressed in sloppy and even indecent clothing, sitting cross-legged or lounging on floors. The counter-revolutionary Catholic does not join this general leveling down in society, but sets a higher standard by presenting himself well.

Likewise, he takes care that his luggage and carry-ons are neat and arranged in an orderly way. Nothing gives a worse impression that broken, ill-kept luggage, or papers and packages falling out of carry-ons.

Other means of traveling

Despite the pleasure that traveling by plane, train, subway or bus may give, it generally imposes a series of sacrifices. By the way he responds to them, a man of poorly formed character reveals himself to the eyes of all. It is not agreeable for anyone to travel with rude and egotistic persons, or those who are extremely touchy and nervous. Shortly one knows the degree of culture of a fellow traveler, be it by his temper, his fastidiousness or the rusticity of ways.

In fact, every trip of some length will reveal the defects of the egotistical, demanding, discourteous. or ill-tempered young man, because a long trip is accompanied by inevitable inconveniences and unforeseen circumstances.

The variety of the countryside, the novelty of the natural beauty, the comfort of the vehicles cannot prevent the inevitable inconveniences encountered in travel: unexpected delays and accidents, bad weather, dirty or poor accommodations, impertinent maids or waiters, bad restaurants, noisy or disagreeable fellow passengers, excessive heat or coldness, the odor of certain persons with poor hygiene, etc.

The amiable and cultured passenger supports these disagreeable elements of travel without manifesting annoyance, complaints, or murmurings. He does make scenes or burden his companions with outbursts of bad humor. When traveling we can often witness actual ferocity in defense of places to sit and commodities. How far removed this is from the forgotten law of courtesy.

The well-educated passenger will observe the following rules when traveling by land or air:

- He respects the reserve of others, and likewise asks that others respect his. After exchanging greetings with a seatmate, if he prefers not to speak, he picks up a book or newspaper, politely indicating the conversation is ended. If the fellow traveler is persistent, he may say, "I' m sorry, but I prefer not to talk right now. I have some reading to do."

- He will not open or close the lights or window before asking his neighbors if is convenient for them.

- He will not put his luggage and packages in places that do not correspond to his place.

- If another passenger is collecting his baggage, he will facilitate the work, assisting him or moving his own things if they are in the way.

- He is considerate of the small amount of space assigned to each passenger in most airplanes, and does not take the whole armrest for himself.

- He does not bring strong-smelling food on board that fills the air around him with pungent or acrid smells. Nor does he remove his shoes and subject fellow travelers to foot odor.

- He will not become difficult, overbearing, or sarcastic in his tone of conversion with other passengers.

- Should delays or inconveniences arise, he will avoid criticizing the authorities, berating the travel company or putting the blame on some particular employee or person.

- Upon arriving at his destination, he will salute his neighboring companions with a quick gesture of acknowledgement.

The correct behavior

For an intelligent young man, the most perfect way to travel is to enter into the quiet reading of a good book or magazine. At the beginning of the trip, the Catholic crosses himself, raises his heart to God and commends his trip to his Guardian Angel. He thinks of the friends or family whom he is leaving and those he is going to meet.

During the trip, he will be composed, amiable, and helpful. If the trip involves meals or a stay in a hotel, he practices both the patience and good manners that are natural to him. He will avoid impertinent remarks to the waitresses and maids, or raising brawls with his travel companions.

While everyone prizes the polite manner and gentility of character of the well-bred, considerate young man, no one likes the company of an egoist, above all on trips. The egoistical passenger is a whip for his companions. He pushes everyone aside in lines. He fusses with his bags and packages as others wait. He occupies his place as if he were traveling alone, having no consideration for others. He does not rise for ladies, the elderly, the handicapped, the sick or children except when he is forced to do so.

In short, he does not try to accommodate anyone. He is immersed in himself and his own inconveniences, which he exaggerates in his mind.

In hotels

In hotels, the egoistical traveler imagines himself the center of the world. He constantly complains at the desk over the smallest matters and makes special demands beyond the ordinary. In the lobby, he calls out to his friends from across the room and feels free to enter into the conversations of everyone.

In the hotel restaurant, he makes loud disparaging remarks about the dishes, he complains at the service, he opens his mouth to clean his teeth, he belches when he drinks, he clicks his teeth on the silverware, he wipes his face with the napkin, in short, he steps on all the rules of good manners.

The braggart fools no one but himself

It is a torture on a trip to find oneself seated next to the vain, presumptuous, and arrogant loud mouth, eager to talk about himself and everything he owns or has accomplished in life. The braggart employs every stratagem to be admired and praised. Simultaneously, he has nothing but complaints about others.

Often he is also a liar, telling a fantastic story of accomplishments he has not accomplished, a prodigious wealth and family possessions he does not possess. In his tiresome tale, he overwhelmed all his teachers with his brilliance, passed every examination with flying colors, knows the great hotels of the principal capitals of the world, won elections against formidable adversaries, or carried out confidential assignments of utmost importance. He is the friend of ministers and diplomats, or perhaps celebrities and movie stars. His automobiles and electronic gadgets are all the latest and best models.

But no one believes what he says. The Catholic gentleman avoids this kind of behavior and always obeys the precepts of courtesy – above all on trips. He gives good example. He is prudent, reserved, discreet, honest, and helpful. He knows that the well-bred man never makes a display of his money or possessions, or discusses his personal finances or private family affairs with others. Only a vulgar braggart speaks about how much this or that cost him.

Fulfillment of religious duties

The Catholic young man does not fear to carry out his religious duties when he travels.

At the beginning of an airplane trip, he will say his travel prayers, asking Our Lady and his guardian angel to protect him and see him safely to his destination. He does not omit his prayers before and after meals served during the trip.

He also does not have human respect to take his Rosary out of his pocket to silently pray it.

Today in our secular and vulgar environments, it can take courage for a young man to make these small religious gestures in public. Such acts reveal a man of character who fears and loves God more than the fickle and always-shifting opinions of man.

Examples

Feeling that the end of his pilgrimage on this earth was approaching, the elder Tobias asked his son, the young Tobias, to undertake a journey to Gabael in Rages of Medina to obtain the 10 tales of silver left in bond by his father. The young man sought a companion for his journey. The Angel Raphael, in human form, presented himself as guide.

The young Tobias walked along confidently because, despite several incidents, he traveled in optimum conditions. On our trips, we should ask the protection of St. Raphael and remember that our companion is our Guardian Angel.

On one occasion Monsieur Louis Martin, the father of St. Therese of Lisieux, found himself in the presence of a poor and hungry epileptic at a railway station who lacked means to purchase a ticket to return to his home some distance away. Mr. Martin was so touched with pity that he took off his hat and placing his own alms in it, proceeded to beg on behalf of the poor man from the passengers to add their contributions. Money poured in, and it was with a heart brimming over with gratitude that the sick man blessed his benefactor.

During our trips, we should practice charity when we can, giving relief to Jesus Christ in His suffering members.

Chapter 21

Proper Behavior for Visiting

Visiting has become a lost art. In our fast-paced world where everyone is rushed, who has time for a visit? In societies where the Catholic spirit reigns, the gentleman will make time for the obligatory social visit. He will also assume the natural duties that impose themselves: visiting the sick, and offering assistance to the poor, the elderly, and widows.

Man is a social creature

Social relations are a necessity for human life and at times, a sweet salve for its troubles. We should leave our homes not only for business and recreation, but also to visit our friends, to tighten relations with relatives, and to fulfill civil and religious duties with the constituted authorities.

The principal events in the life of the family – births, baptisms, First Communion, marriages, anniversaries, or deaths – are other occasions when our relatives are grateful to receive moral and spiritual expressions of support and amity by our sincere participation in the joys and sorrows of life.

Young children should not make visits unless they are accompanied by some other person of their family. The time for the visit should be established in advance and correspond to the convenience of the person visited.

In small towns and among related persons or close friends, it is sufficient to dress in one's daily attire. Today, because of our bad customs, it is necessary to note that daily attire should always be dignified, clean, and modest. For example, a young man should not visit his grandmother in sports shorts and a T-shirt. On other more formal occasions or when visiting persons outside the familiar circle, he should present himself well dressed, in accordance with the circumstances. If the reception is ceremonious, a suit and tie should be worn.

The calling card of the past

In the past, there was the charming custom of the calling card. Some of our young readers may have never even heard of such a thing. This European-style custom was followed in some cities of the United States even until the 1950s or '60s, when the Law of the Casual began to impose its despotic reign everywhere. Nonetheless, with the hope that some day such customs might be revived, we record the briefest summary of the workings of the calling card.

It was customary for a visitor to present oneself at the door, and leave a calling card with the maid, who placed it on a table in the vestibule. There were strict rules governing the card's size and the engraving. If, after some rings, no one appeared at the door, the visitor would leave his calling card at the doorway.

When a maid or doorman appeared, the visitor would ask, "Is Mr. X or Mrs. Y available?" If the response were affirmative, the person entered and accompanied the maid to the visitors' hall. The hat and the overcoat, as well as the umbrella or cane, were always left in the vestibule. Once in the salon, if left alone, the visitor took a correct attitude, avoiding touching objects, pictures, albums, photographs, the piano, and so on. In the days of the ceremonious reception, the young man would kiss the hand of the lady of the house should she appear.

If the response were negative, he did not insist. He left his visiting card, writing some few amiable words on it expressing his regret for having missed the person.

The art of presentation

Entering a room where many other guests or persons of the house are seated, the visitor shakes hands with his host or hostess, makes a slight inclination of greeting to the others present, and gives a handshake to the men he knows. Then, with all calm, he will take a seat, avoiding choosing the most comfortable unless he is invited to do so. This maneuver of entering a salon demands experience and confidence, which are the supreme rules.

Those accustomed to society know the art of presentation. From youth, a boy should learn to conquer his natural timidity that can make him awkward in social situations. Once he enters the room and acknowledges the hostess, he should know how to enter into conversations naturally with those around him. At a small gathering, the host or hostess will introduce the guests to each other. This is not done on formal occasions when a great many persons are present. To be invited to be under a friend's roof is already supposed to be an introduction to those it shelters.

In small gatherings, it is necessary for the youth to rise each time a lady or an elderly person enters the room, or if someone comes to him to present his farewell.

It would be discourteous at a social gathering, visit, or reception in a private home to not speak with the others present or to assume a severe, glacial, or pedantic attitude. This could cause discomfort to the host or other visitors. Likewise, it is disagreeable to be too familiar. One of the worst habits is to pat, nudge, or take hold of people when conversing with them.

If by chance two persons who have estranged relations meet at the same gathering, the one who arrived last should retire discreetly after a short while, without raising notice. It is always bad taste to let others know that enmities exist against us in society, and in particular we should keep this veiled from the eyes of the one we are visiting.

A young man's language should always be respectful, as elegant as possible, and circumspect, revealing that he is well-bred. Street terms and expressions, a general sign of vulgar ways and lack of politesse, should never be used among ladies and gentlemen.

To know how to listen

Reserve and circumspection will save one's reputation from irreparable shipwreck. The young man who knows how to listen and reflect before speaking will certainly be amiably accepted in society. A youth should listen and learn from those with more courteous and fine forms of language, and then follow their good example. He should avoid the imperious and arrogant tones that cool friendships and raise antipathies.

During a visit or amiable gathering, discussions that are too lively and sharp should be avoided. A visit is not a debating hall. A veil of amiability should be drawn over all expositions of ideas and facts. A cultured man knows how to show interest in the conversation of those present and to contribute to it at opportune times with his reserve of knowledge. If he does not know anything about a topic, he should remain silent. Only the fool enters into literary or scientific jousts without the proper training or knowledge.

Avoid the open contradiction of, strong censure of, or gossip about those who are not there. It is cowardice to attack an absent person who cannot defend himself or retaliate

Discussions: the schools of friendship

In friendships, a man should have the right to hold his opinions and maintain his personal independence. It is natural to expose your thoughts and the reasons for your way of thinking. Your character should manifest itself in every action of life. Not even the bonds of friendship demand forced neutrality on important topics and abdication of personality.

The most slippery or treacherous ground in conversation is the religious or political discussion. At social gatherings, one should not head in that direction without good reason. In those cases when the topic is raised, it is normal to affirm your convictions, being aware that probably no one will change his political opinion or religious belief because of the discussion. A discussion on religion, however, can be the way that Divine Providence desires to work to convert persons to the Catholic Faith. For this reason, a youth should become familiar with the main principles of Catholic doctrine appropriate for the present day needs. A person should never speak about what he does not know. Nor should he approve what he does not understand or what seems wrong.

When to end a visit

In general, the duration of visit should not exceed 20 to 30 minutes, except if it is among relatives or close friends. The person who knows how to end a visit at a convenient moment before his presence becomes inopportune is appreciated as pleasant company.

Upon leaving, the visitor should rise, say some amiable words, and retire without haste. If the gathering is small, he should express his thanks to the host and hostess, making a slight bow. At many gatherings, above all at larger parties, it is permitted to retire without taking leave of the host and hostess, unless they are particularly sensitive to the testimony of that deference. It would be taken as rude to leave at the exact moment that other visitors enter. It is convenient to remain several minutes with them before taking one's leave.

After announcing his intention to leave, the guest should do so. The long drawn-out exit is tiresome for both the host and other visitors.

Conversation

If a man is speaking about his wife, a family member, or friend in the presence of those who do not know them, he should not omit the convenient qualification. For example, he would say "My wife Louise ..." If the company knows her, he should simply refer to her as Louise. He should never refer to his wife as "Mrs. X."

A well-mannered man will try to be amiable when conversing with others, expressing real interest in them and steering them toward conversations on themes that are agreeable to them.

No one should dominate the conversation, try to direct or close a discussion, pronounce judgments in an authoritarian tone, or attempt to sparkle like a star on stage. Young men should take care not to fall into such faults, which reveal a thin veneer of culture and little skill in communicating with one's fellow man.

Respect for the feelings of others, prudence, and Catholic charity oblige us to an extreme reserve in choosing our words. The courteous man says nothing without thinking first, nor does he say everything that he is thinking. Imprudence in this matter can be fatal to a friendship. Haste in speaking can cause profound humiliations.

Here are several true stories to illustrate the point. The reader can certainly add his own anecdotes involving irreparable social gaffes made by speakers who did not weigh their words.

During a large gathering, one military man asked another, "Since you're in the Fourth Division, surely you know Colonel X?"

The new acquaintance replied: "I know him very well. As proof, I can attest he is a perfect brute to those under his command."

The first officer responded, somewhat coldly, "He's my brother."

This is the result of speaking without thinking ...

At a dance given in a private home, a young man approached another man who was standing idly by, looking somewhat bored. He said to him, "I'm sick and tired of this boring party. I'm leaving. Do you want to come with me?"

The man answered, "You have my permission to go. I'm the owner of this house."

It is doubtful our young artless fellow received another invitation to that house.

At a debutante party, one young man asked another gentleman in dress uniform, "Who is that lady over there in the cream-colored dress with the moon face?"

"It's my wife."

"You misunderstood me," said the unfortunate youth, his face red with shame, "I wanted to say that lady in blue, near the one in cream."

"Oh, that's my sister," the man replied.

The list of incidents like this has no end.

Social obligations and business visits

Even when they are tiresome, when they are not motivated by friendship, visits are a social obligation. They favor peace and harmony among men. They embellish life; they dispel loneliness; they give comfort in sorrow. They elevate ways of being; they perfect customs; they create urbanity.

In small towns or rural areas, visits are more familiar, losing the more ceremonious tone of the great cities, and can be longer. Then the visitor is always invited to take the indispensable coffee or tea.

Visits that businessmen make in seeking clientele obey the various rules of the area. The result of his proposals frequently bears a direct relation to the way he presents himself and his products. He should expose his topic with clarity and brevity, without fastidious digressions or tiring the listener with long spiels or tall tales. He should be quick to listen without interrupting the responses of the one he addresses. If his proposal is unsuccessful, he should take his leave amiably, thus leaving with the hope of receiving a more favorable response at another opportunity.

This polite behavior leaves a good impression on the one who has given his time to hear the proposal. He will privately praise the courtesy of the salesman and not resent having given his time; further, he will be more disposed to receive him again sometime in the future.

The courteous host and guest

When a person is a guest in our home for some time, he has the right to a special treatment. The guest, says the proverb, is the blessing of God.

Without having given advance notice or having been invited, a person should not present himself to receive lodging at the house of a friend. It is very arrogant, crackling with incivility and impertinence, to invite oneself to the house of another unless there are serious and obvious reasons for doing so, based on a long-standing friendship or close family relations.

Cordiality and discretion summarize the code of duties of the one who receives as well as the one who is received. To invite someone to be your houseguest is to assure his well-being for the time that he passes under your roof. Therefore, whoever receives a guest should show him every attention. On the other hand, the one invited should accept such attentions with a certain reserve, taking care not to abuse the hospitality of his host.

The host should make every attempt to meet his guest at the airport or station. The room and bath facilities should be ready and very clean. The host should take care to show the guest the general layout of the house, his bed, bathroom, drinking water, lights, and other amenities, as well as inform him the time for meals and the general schedule of the house. He should not let the guest know if his presence is causing some member of the family an inconvenience or upsetting the house schedule.

The host should allow the guest the comfort of some hours alone each day, to go out for a walk or remain in his room, depending on the quarters of the house. For certain persons, solitude for special private occupations – reading, letter-writing, prayers, and so on - constitutes a necessity in his way of life.

The guest should show himself satisfied with everything that is done for him. He should avoid complaining or looking vexed, even if he lacks something. The cultured guest does not involve himself in the affairs of the household; he closes his ears and eyes to the less edifying things he may see or hear. It is a complete lack of gratitude to criticize his host's household and affairs to others.

The polite guest does not take too literally the warm invitation to "treat my house as if it were your own," but is careful to respect the customs of the household. The guest should take breakfast following the schedule of the house. He should avoid rising either too early or too late, smoking in the rooms, coming in very late at night, and so on.

The considerate guest will leave on the pre-determined day despite any insistence made to keep him. Such requests are a courtesy to which one responds with another courtesy. On the day of departure, it is appropriate to offer some small gift to the lady of the house or the children to express gratitude for the hospitality and the attentions given. Some days after leaving, the guest will remember to send a letter thanking those who treated him as a member of the family.

St. Anthony's visit to St. Paul the Hermit

Note how the hermit St. Paul received the visit of St. Anthony.

Both were living in Egypt. Paul was 113-years-old and had been living alone in a cave in the desert for 60 years. Anthony, age 90, was living in a monastery in the desert and thought that he was the oldest hermit in the world.

In order to correct this beginning of vanity, God revealed to St. Anthony the existence of a man who was older and holier than he, and ordered him to seek Paul out and visit him. Anthony put his confidence in God, set out in the desert, and walked for two days and two nights until Providence led him to the cell of Paul.

The latter, seeing himself discovered, closed himself in his cave. Anthony did not leave, but prayed until the hermit decided to appear. After a long wait, the door opened. Paul came out and the two saints embraced. Despite the fact they had never seen each other, they addressed each other by name.

"You have found the one you have sought, my brother," Paul told Anthony. "You are seeing a man who in a short time will be dust and ashes." Then he asked his guest questions about the persecution of the Christians and the state of things in the world, to which Anthony responded as best he could.

While they spoke, a crow came and brought a whole loaf of bread. Seeing this, Paul, filled with admiration, exclaimed, "See how good and merciful God is, sending us this food. For the 60 years I have been here, daily I have received a half loaf of bread. Because of your visit, today God sends us a whole loaf."

The two saints thanked Divine Providence and passed the rest of the day and night in pious colloquy and prayer.

The next morning, Paul said to his companion, "For some time I have known that you lived in this vicinity. Since I am at the end of my life, God has sent you here to bury my body."

Saddened to hear this, Anthony begged the holy hermit that he take him to Heaven with him.

"This is not the will of God," responded Paul. "You must continue on this earth for some time in order to direct the religious in your monastery. Now, go and return with the mantle that you received from St. Athanasius so that you can wrap my dead body in it."

He made this request to prevent Anthony from witnessing his death, as well as to show his great respect for the intrepid Bishop Athanasius.

When Anthony returned to the religious of his monastery, he told them, "Woe to me, poor sinner that I am! I do not deserve the name of religious. I have seen Elias, I have seen St. John Baptist in the desert. I have seen Paul in paradise."

Taking the mantle of Athanasius, he hurried back to the cave. On the road he caught sight of the soul of the saint surrounded by light rising up to Heaven in the company of the Angels, Prophets, and Apostles.

Chapter 21

Upon entering the cave, he found Paul on his knees, immovable, his arms stretched out in a cross, and his head turned toward Heaven. He seemed to be praying, but he was no longer living.

Anthony wrapped the body in the mantle of St. Athanasius. To help dig the grave, two lions came out of the neighboring forest, stopped before the cadaver, and then dug a hole in the sand sufficient to bury the body. Anthony prayed over the dead body and buried it. Before returning to his monastery, Anthony took Paul's tunic made of palm leaves. For him it was a precious relic that he wore on great feast days.

Chapter 22

Writing Letters

In this age of fast messaging with e-mails and other electronic devices, the art of letter-writing is being lost. This is most unfortunate. Every well-bred young man should know how to write a letter, and have the proper writing materials to do so. There is no substitute for the handwritten thank-you letter, condolence letter, or nicely scripted invitation, acceptance, or regret.

The letter

The letter is a written conversation, realized through space and time. It should be a genuine expression of the mind and heart.

The essential quality of a letter is authenticity, in expression as well as general style. This quality and a good tone reveal the character and culture of the one who writes, just as a badly written letter is a testimony of an uncultured man.

Presentation is important

The letter you write is always a mirror that reflects your appearance, taste, and character. A sloppy letter with bad spelling, slanting lines, and perhaps even a blot or two reveals the kind of person who is messy, disordered, and undisciplined. A neat finely written letter, on the other hand, is most likely from the hand of the orderly and well disciplined young man.

The best external adornment of a letter is simple, clean, good quality paper that is properly formatted. That is, the top and bottom of the paper and a left margin should be left blank.

If a letter extends to four pages, the writing on each page should be vertical; do not use extravagant styles such as alternating the pages with horizontal and vertical writing. Another bad habit is to scrawl extra notes anywhere on the pages. These can be present in your draft, but not in the final letter. If two pages are insufficient, add another page with the appropriate number in the upper right hand corner. There no need to number the first page.

If a boy has difficulty writing in a straight line, he can place a lined paper under his stationary in order to keep his handwriting even and straight. If this recourse does not work, it is acceptable to use a lined writing paper. The sender should be aware, however, that a lined paper considerably diminishes the level of a letter.

Writing paper for a man should be conservative. Plain white, gray and granite are the normal colors acceptable. It reveals good taste and appreciation for your correspondent to have your paper engraved with your full name. Before the age of computers, such stationary was made in special printing houses with fine, elaborate fonts and embossed lettering. Today, one can make a very acceptable stationary using the home computer.

The practice of engraving the person's name varies according to cultural customs. In the United States the engraving is generally placed on the top center of the page; in European countries it is on the top left.

The ink color should be blue or black for men. Today the ballpoint pen has invaded everywhere, and is also admitted in formal letters. If, however, you are writing to someone who knows and appreciates the old forms, use a fountain pen. It will earn you his respect.

The envelope should harmonize with the paper. Do not use varied colors, for example, a red envelope with white paper.

Letters should be properly dated. Usually the date is put at the upper right hand of the first page of a letter, or at the end and to the left of the signature in a note. The date should be written March 3, 2008, and not 3-3-08.

A letter should be written with a good, legible handwriting. An undecipherable letter is discourteous because it shows that one prizes neither the time nor the patience of the reader. The letters should be well-formed in a script hand, giving proper height to the letters l, b, d, and f, and not omitting any punctuation mark.

To have a clean, well-composed letter, follow the wise practice of writing a first draft. Then, after re-reading it and making changes and corrections, pen the final letter in a neat hand. This good custom should be taken up from a young age, and continued as an adult.

Once your letter is ready, carefully make a single or double fold depending on the format of the paper and envelope, but in such a way that first page of the letter is on the inside rather than the outside of a letter of more than one page. A letter loses much of its good first effect by a sloppy folding job.

Addressing the envelope merits special attention, not only so that the letter arrives at the proper place, but also because it will make the first good – or bad – impression on the one receiving it. Take care, then, to write the address in an exact and very legible hand.

It is always possible to improve

As a young man, Marshal Ferdinand Foch, who commanded the Allied armies in France in World War I, had a terrible handwriting. However, paying heed to the advice given him, he came to write so neatly that his letters seemed typed. One can see that this great Catholic man did not admit the formula "I can't."

Style and content

What we have said until now, while rigorously pragmatic, is only the wrapping of the package. Inside is the gift: the sentiments and thoughts that one person wants to reveal to another.

The supreme rule is to consider the person to whom one is writing: the age, authority, social position and relationship to the writer. Keeping this in mind and the matter being addressed, the letter will burgeon naturally, relying on your sense of propriety and good manners.

That is to say, if a youth is addressing an authority, such as a priest or professor, he should maintain a formal and polite tone. Speaking to his grandmother or uncle, he may use a warmer style, but should keep the respectful and courteous manner in writing. In addressing letters to his friends, he may assume a more informal style, but he should never use slang or the vulgar expressions so common among youth today. This is particularly important in letters addressed to ladies.

Prolix and pretentious phrases should be avoided. Instead of impressing, the writer only appears ostentatious and vainglorious.

Always remember that the wounds that come from the pen from rude and uncivil language are gashes from the sword. They can leave indelible scars on the soul. And they can be mortal to a friendship.

Exercising prudence in what you say in letters is the safeguard of friendships. Even in a letter that expresses disapproval, the terms should be imbued with gentility. It is good to compose one's words in a letter in such a way that it could be read not only by one to whom it is addressed, but also by other persons. In general a letter should contain nothing that does not merit public display. The same care should be taken with regard to e-mails.

The salutations, letter form, and closings are things taught in elementary school. A good teacher makes an effort to develop a proper letter style in his students.

Formal addresses and closings

Here are some samples of written salutations and closings that were used in the past in formal letters. It is advisable to revive the practice of more formal and respectful salutations and closings.

To the Pope:

Written Address: The Sovereign Pontiff, Your Holiness Pius XII.

Letter Salutation: Your Holiness Pius XII,

Formal Closing: On my knees before Your Holiness, protesting my filial dedication and imploring the favor of an apostolic blessing, I have the honor to be,

    The humble and obedient Servant of Your Holiness,
    (Signature)

To a Cardinal:

Written Address: His Eminence, Thomas Cardinal Stand, Archbishop of Los Angeles

Letter Salutation: Your Eminence,

Formal Closing: Be pleased to accept the homage of profound respect with which I have the honor to offer you as,

    The humble and dedicated servant of Your Eminence,
    (Signature)

For an Archbishop or Bishop, the same formula can be employed with the substitution of His Excellency and Your Excellency for His Eminence and Your Eminence.

To a person of high station or stature:

Written Address: The Hon. John Glover Roberts, Jr.

Written Salutation: Dear Sir, or Sir,

Formal Closing: I ask Your Excellency (Your Honor) to accept my profound respect. I remain

    Your humble and obedient servant,
    Or, I have the honor to remain,
      Yours faithfully,
      (Signature)

To all priests or religious, use formulas such as:

Written Address: The Reverend Father John W. Butler, The Reverend Mother Ann Francis, O.S.B., or Sister Anthony Christine, O.P.

Letter Salutation: Dear Father, or Dear Rev. Mother,

Formal Closing: Receive the expression of my respect,

Or, Receive my sentiments of filial respect,

Or, Offering my respectful homage,

Or, Most respectfully,

  (Signature)

To a person of medium dignity, close:

With great respect and consideration, I remain,

Or, Most respectfully,

Or, Most faithfully,

  (Signature)

Between persons of equal or almost equal status, close:

Offering my consideration and esteem, I have the pleasure to be,

Your attentive and grateful friend (or colleague),

Or, Sincerely,

Or, Faithfully,

  (Signature)

To closer friends or relatives, close:

I have the great satisfaction to sign myself,

Your loyal friend,

Or , Your devoted grandson,

  (Signature)

For a parent:

I close, signing with the greatest respect,

  Your loving and obedient son,

    (Signature)

Chapter 23

Table Manners Reveal a Man's Culture

Many young men find themselves ill at ease at fine restaurants or banquet dinners. They are clumsy, awkward, embarrassed. Why? Because they are not sure about what to do with the line-up of silverware and the row of glasses. The uncomfortable youth butters a slice of bread and then realizes that others are breaking off a piece at a time and buttering it individually. He blows on the soup to cool it and wonders why eyebrows raise. In short, he is missing the knowledge and self-assurance that are the fruit of good table manners practiced daily.

The best time to learn good table manners is as a youth at the family table, but it is never too late to start. The man who strives to achieve Catholic perfection is always eager to refine himself in all things, including his table manners.

The Golden Rule

The adroit and prudent young man knows how to cover for any possible shortcomings in his manners. There is, however, a particular moment when these inadequacies reveal themselves more clearly – it is the hour of meals taken in the company of others.

One's posture, gestures, manner of eating, and relations maintained with others at the table are visible and sure criteria to determine a person's degree of culture. At meals one reveals whether he is accustomed to dine politely or is ignorant of general table etiquette.

Since the table is where one meets persons of the family and society, the laws of the table are important. The Golden Rule is expressed in two forms: avoid showing any discontent with what is served, and try to please one's neighbor as much as it is fitting, without making overblown eulogies or telling lies. Superlatives, such as "This is the best roasted chicken I have ever had in my life" and other such overstatements, are cheap resources to please and shine that often produce the opposite effect. Be polite, but stay within the limits of the truth.

Catholic hospitality and the sincere desire of both host and guest to please one another constitute the principal elements that inspired table customs, and even the invention of many table utensils and items. Let us enter into some details on this topic.

Being punctual

Punctuality is a factor of order and harmony. Delay causes disorder in the daily schedule and work, causes inconvenience to others at the table, and disconcerts the cook.

At formal dinner parties, the rule is to arrive five minutes early, so as to greet the members of the house and other guests. A delay is not justified, even by the most skillfully prepared excuse.

The rule is to foresee possible problems on the road in order to be able to arrive on time. If problems are anticipated, it is better to start some time earlier. Then, if no difficulties are encountered, one can find a place to sit and read, or pass a short time until the appointed hour.

Some persons wrongly imagine that to be late is a sign of one's importance. Do not fall into this error. It is a discourtesy that only serves to disturb the dinner schedule, and will impress no one. The same rule that informs the guest to be punctual, tells the host to wait no more than 10 or 15 minutes to begin the planned meal. The host who follows good protocol will not change the sequence of courses to accommodate the late guest. It is the latecomer who must risk having his place at the table taken by another person, losing the appetizer and first course, and being the general cause of irritation to the entire party. We see that to be late does not promote anyone socially; rather it does the opposite.

At the table

At the dining table, the guest will occupy the place indicated to him, and will seat himself only after the host or head of the table is seated.

He will greet, if he has not already done so, the persons around him and will discreetly enter into conversation, guarding his words. Conversation at a formal dinner should be turned to cordial small talk, until a common subject of interest is found. When one is sure that his neighbor agrees with him on a particular topic, then a more open exchange of ideas may take place.

Are discussions allowed? This depends on the group of persons invited to the dinner, as well as the nature of the party. At the family table, in a circle of close friends, or at a social club, it is normal to have exchanges of ideas and opinions, insofar as respect and amiability are maintained. At a table with unknown persons, such as at a formal banquet, such discussions should be avoided. It is also disagreeable to have to listen to others proselytizing at a meal.

Avoid reports on one's health, especially if prosaic details are involved. Should you dine with an older person suffering from well-known ailments, a short and courteous: "How is that bad ankle of yours?" or "Are you recovering well from your surgery?" suffices. The table is not the appropriate place to discuss medical problems and prescriptions.

Instead of trying to dominate the conversation, a young man will listen with interest to the topic of conversation chosen by the guests of honor or the head of the table.

If he has some point to raise, he should frame it as a question to the one speaking, remembering that elders like to be asked their advice or opinions. After his question is answered, he can enter easily into the conversation as an accepted party either asking another question or offering his opinion, without, however, appearing pretentious.

As he follows or joins in the conversation, he will keep an eye on what is going on with his neighbors with the aim of helping them if they need something. This should be a point of special attention if his table neighbors are elderly persons or ladies.

Unless he is at a restaurant or a club with close friends, he should not call a waiter from across the room. However he can take advantage of when the waiter passes to ask for the desired items.

Table settings

A disconcerting sight for the inexperienced dinner guest at a formal dinner is the array of glasses and silverware he faces at his place setting. It is not, however, as mysterious as it appears. The general rule to follow is simple: eating utensils are used from the outside in. Use a new utensil for each course (don't save your salad fork to use with the main course, for instance). When you don't know what utensil to use, watch what your host does and follow suit.

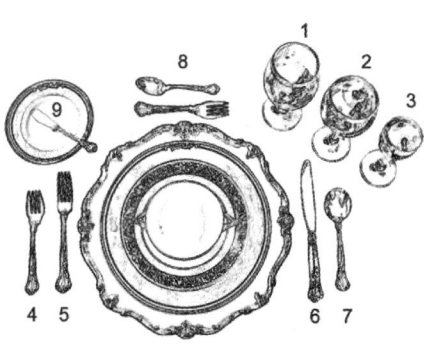

The silverware at left is arranged for a three course meal and dessert: first, the salad course (salad fork, 4); second, the soup course (soup spoon, 7); third, the meat course (fork and knife, 5 and 6), and the dessert (dessert fork and spoon, 8). The smaller bread knife (9) is placed across the bread plate positioned at the upper left of the plate.

The water goblet (1), the largest, is placed above the knives.

To its right and slightly in front of it is the red wine glass (2) or the smaller white wine glass (3).

In the picture *below,* one finds the formal banquet place setting, which is set European style, that is, with the salad as the last course instead of the first. Therefore, the salad fork is next to the plate. There is a reason for this: it allows the diner to enjoy the fullest taste of the wines served with the fish and meat plates. Because the salad vinegar can affect the palate and change the taste of the wine, the salad comes after the main course instead of before it.

This picture shows a setting for a five-course meal and dessert: the first, the shellfish plate (seafood or oyster fork, 11), the soup course (soup spoon, 10), the fish course (fish fork and knife, 5 and 9), the meat course (dinner fork and knife, 6 and 8), the salad (salad fork, 7), and the dessert (dessert fork and spoon, 12). The butter knife (13) is set across the butter plate at left.

The glasses include the water glass (1) to the extreme left, followed by the champagne glass (2) placed a little behind the others since the champagne is served at the dessert, and then the red wine (3) and white wine (4) glasses, placed according to size to allow the diner easy reach. If the dinner is served by waiters, they will remove the white wine glasses with the fish plates and the red wine glasses with the meat plates, leaving only the water and the champagne glasses for the dessert.

There are two acceptable ways to use a knife and fork: American style and European style. In the American style, one holds the knife in the right hand, and fork in the left. Cut a piece of meat, then place the knife on the edge of your plate (with the blade facing in), then switch your fork to your right hand to eat (unless, of course, you are left-handed).

In the European style, hold the knife in your right hand, the fork in the left. You do not switch hands - you eat with your fork in your left hand.

It is amazing how many youths today do not know the most elementary table etiquette: the correct way to hold the fork. The proper way is to balance the utensil between the first knuckle of the middle finger and the tip of the index finger, while using the thumb to support the handle. When you use a knife, the tip of your index finger should rest on the upper blade of the knife. Never hold the utensil in a full-fisted way.

Begin eating only after everyone at the table has been served.

The placement of flatware when not in use acts as a message to the well-educated host or waiter, allowing the diner to indicate whether he has paused in eating, will eat more, or has finished the plate. When a guest finishes his salad and soup, the salad fork and the soup spoon should be set across the plates. If you would like another serving of soup, place the top of your spoon (concave side down) on the edge of the plate, with its handle setting on the table. At formal dinners it is not advisable to ask for a second helping because such requests will delay the service schedule.

When a guest finishes eating the fish and meat courses, he signals this by setting the fork and knife parallel to each other, either across the center of the plate or diagonally with the handles pointing to the right. The cutting edge of the knife faces the diner and the fork tines are preferably up.

If the diner has not finished, he indicates this by setting the fork on the left and the knife on the right so that they cross over each other in the center of the plate. The diner preparing to pass his plate for a second helping places the fork and knife parallel to each other at the right side of the plate, so that there is room for the food.

The good waiter will know how to distinguish these codes, and never ask the stupid question: "Are you still working on this?" When the guest does not know these rules, the polite waiter will approach with the tray to ask: "Will you accept a little more?" or inquire "May I take your plate?"

The general rule for serving, easily memorized, is: *serve left and remove from the right.* That is with food. As far as beverages, you serve them from the right. At a dinner with several courses, the used plate and corresponding silverware and wine glass are removed from the right. If a guest is still enjoying the wine served with that course, the glass should be left on the table.

At a formal dinner or banquet, food should be presented to guests in the following order: guest of honor, female guests, male guests, hostess, host. At restaurants, the meals are generally served first to the women, then to the men, with the older served before the younger.

During the meal, the standard practice is to pass to the right. The salt and pepper should be passed together.

When the meal is finished, fold your napkin neatly and set it to the right of the plate.

The meal table is no place for a purse or briefcase or other personal belongings. Personal effects should be placed on the floor, your lap, or hung on the chair. An exception to this rule is when the lady has a very small banquet purse, which she may set on the table at her right side, next to the silverware. If you have a cell phone with you, be sure it is turned off and placed out of sight. It is a breach of consideration to answer your cell phone during a meal. In the event of an emergency, apologize beforehand for having to answer your phone, then leave the table and talk outside of the room.

Some Essential Table Manners

Table customs differ with every country and epoch. Nonetheless, there are some general rules that are observed everywhere. Here are few rules applicable to all times and places:

At a restaurant or club, if a plate is not satisfactory, you may request the waiter to change it once. If the dish does not please you the second time, do not ask for another replacement. Just remember not to ask for that dish again in the future, or avoid eating at that particular place.

One should not blow on the soup when it is very hot, but should stir it moderately with the spoon. Fill your soup spoon by placing it in the bowl and moving it away from you. You may tilt your bowl away from you to get the last bits of soup, but only do it twice.

The hillbilly keeps hold of his fork; the educated man uses it only to bring the food to his mouth, and then lets it rest on the plate. Remember proper table manners forbid placing a used eating utensil back on the table, where it could soil the tablecloth.

Meats with bones, such as chicken or ribs, can cause difficulty at times. It is not advisable to use your fingers to eat them. One should remove as much meat as possible from them with the knife and fork, and set the bones on one side of the plate, avoiding letting any bones or bits fall on the tablecloth or floor.

The best and safest procedure to follow at the table is to never use your fingers. Exceptions to this rule are for grapes, cherries, tangerines, or the like served as a dessert or appetizer. In this case, the host will often provide a small water bowl for each guest or a wet napkin to clean the fingers.

Difficult food to pick up with the fork, such as peas, can be pushed onto the fork either by the knife or a piece of bread broken off for this purpose. Do not use your fingers.

In the United States, certain foods, such as corn on the cob, spareribs, chicken, sandwiches, and certain fruits are often eaten with the fingers at the table. In Europe and South America, this is not acceptable. In their fine restaurants, the American is always spotted by these less gracious eating habits. It is advisable to follow the more refined customs developed by Christian Civilization, and exercise the discipline of not using the fingers to eat, but rather the proper utensils.

Some other good customs

Good manners prohibit smashing the vegetables on the plate. Except in very familiar company, no one should wipe the plate with bread to absorb the gravy. Even at the family table, children should learn not to do this. Instead, pieces of bread can be put on the plate to take up the gravy, and raised to the mouth with the fork. Gravy should never be eaten with a spoon. The same rules apply to poached or over-easy eggs. Unless you are among close friends or relatives, do not dip your bread into the yolk or smash your egg with the fork. At the family table, you may dip a piece of bread into the yolk and raise it to the mouth, taking care not to spill it on your suit or tie.

Proper etiquette says you should cut only the piece of meat or food that you plan to eat. Do not cut your food up all at one time, unless you are about to feed a baby. Also, it is not advisable for a person to play with his food, arranging and re-arranging it on the plate between bites.

One should eat the salad with the proper fork, taking care not to let pieces escape from the edges of the plate. Use the salad fork, and not a knife, to cut the lettuce. This practice may appear insignificant, but really spotlights a polished person. The considerate host who knows this rule will take care to serve a salad that is manageable with a fork.

Break off small pieces of bread into bite size pieces with the fingers, and not with the knife. Take a portion of butter from the butter dish with your butter knife and place it onto your bread plate. Use the butter that you have placed on your butter plate to butter your bread a piece at a time, not the whole slice at once.

Elementary etiquette demands that you always keep your mouth closed while you chew and do not make loud noises while eating. It's acceptable to talk with a small piece of food in your mouth, but do not attempt it if your mouth is full or close to it.

Always use a napkin to remove leftovers of food from your lips.

The pits of olives, prunes, or any other fruits should be set at the side of the plate. To remove the pit, the general rule is to take it out the same way it went in. So, if you ate the cherry with your fingers, you can remove the pit with your fingers as well, but do so as discreetly as possible. A tasteful way to retrieve a pit is to cup the free hand, then transfer the pit from the mouth to the cupped hand. Open the hand to place the pit on the plate. If you eat an olive in the salad with your fork, deposit the pit on the fork as unobtrusively as possible to return it to the plate.

After removing the skin and seeds, cut an apple or pear into smaller parts and raise them to the mouth with the fork, not with the fingers. A well-bred man cuts his apple or pear from top to bottom, not from side to side.

Oranges are eaten in various ways. The most refined way is to peel the fruit with a fruit knife and fork, cut it into quarters or wedges, and raise them to the mouth with a fork.

At the table, never clean your teeth with your fingers. It is permissible to cover the mouth with one hand, avert the face slightly, and remove the food with a toothpick as inconspicuously as possible. A sure sign of a hillbilly is the person who leaves the table or restaurant with a toothpick hanging out of his mouth.

These rules and many others that should govern table habits are not arbitrary. They are the fruit of experience, and their objective is the well-being, pleasure, and dignity of everyone at the table, and to maintain the best order in clothing and utensils.

Drinks and coffee

The *aperitif,* from the Latin *aperire,* is a wine or alcoholic drink to open the appetite. Vermouth, sherry, port, or a light wine are often served before a meal, usually with a light appetizer such as crackers or olives. A tomato juice cocktail is a nonalcoholic drink that is commonly served as an *aperitif.* Europeans also serve a *digestif* after meals, which is usually a strong dry spirit for men and a liqueur for women. Port or Sherry may also be served after meals.

All drinks should be served in an appropriate vessel. Never drink water, beer, or a soft drink from a bottle or can; ask for a glass.

When pouring wine, beer, or any other drink, it is proper to hold the bottle by the higher part, rather than the lower.

It is necessary to accustom children to drink silently, without making slurping or other sounds. One should drink slowly and not when one has food in the mouth.

At company meals, the toast should be simple and short, joyful, and good humored. At such meals the guest waits until the toast is made before beginning to drink from his wine or champagne glass. At banquets or ceremonial dinners, the toast is made at the beginning of the dessert, the right hand slightly raised. Traditionally, at a formal dinner the host or hostess offers the first toast. If a speech is delivered, it should be made during the dessert. This is a polite way to insinuate that it should be short, since both the homage and the thank-you responses should not take longer than the dessert. The toasting glass should be only half-filled at maximum.

The toast should always be responded to. A speech does not require any response from the guest of honor except a simple "Thank you."

Physical nourishment may be accompanied by a spiritual refreshment. In religious communities, a public reading from edifying works during meals ennobles the meal activity. In the family home, calm, unpretentious, and pleasant conversation will make the meal into a human act, and not just feeding the body its required nutrients. It is a lack of civility to watch television or read papers or books when dining with others at the table.

Finally, no one should forget that sobriety and moderation protect health of body and soul. The wise man is the temperate man who lives a longer and better life. To know how to live is a requisite for living long, harmonic years.

The Shah and the asparagus

At times it is necessary to exercise presence of mind to help a neighbor and prevent him from some public infraction of basic table manners. When a foreigner or one new to our customs is lost in the confusion of an invincible ignorance, it is charitable to help him or to take a measure to save him from some humiliation. Here is a case like this.

In 1873 the Prince of Wales, the future Edward VII, King of England, invited the Shah of Persia to lunch in London with a group of notable personalities. The Shah was not accustomed to European habits. When he was served a plate of asparagus with a savory sauce, he picked up a piece between his fingers, dipped it in the sauce, tilted his head back, lowered the asparagus into it, and sucked off the outer layer and sauce. Then, with the greatest naturality in the world, he threw the remainder to the side of the chair.

There was a silent but general stupefaction at the table.

The Prince of Wales, without a moment of hesitation, did the same. Then all the guests imitated him. The servants did not know where such an unexpected bombardment of asparagus stems came from!

Chapter 24

Reading and Speech-Making

To give our social relations the tone of courtesy that should always characterize them, it is necessary to read, write, and speak not only with proper grammar, but also with the elegance and perfection required for the cultural and social milieus that we frequent. It is not enough to have attended college for many years or to have many titles to know how to read or speak in public. There are highly educated men who lack such skills. It is necessary *first*, to know how to read profitably, and *second,* to know how to read aloud and speak well to please others.

Knowing how to read

Before knowing how to read in public, it is indispensable to know how to read in private. The good cook will serve his friends plates that he has prepared before and personally likes. So also, the reader who likes the material he is presenting will communicate easily and naturally. If he dislikes the topic or has never seen it before, the reading is artificial and lacks the power of persuasion.

How does one read well? It is impossible to read properly with the radio or television blaring. The good reader recollects himself in the intimacy of his room, in the silence of the morning or the quiet of the evening, removing himself from the affairs of the world.

The good book communicates to us the Catholic thinking of men of valor who have lived in other times in diverse countries. It is advisable to take notes while reading, jotting down the pages with passages that impress or move us so that they are readily accessible in the future. Some young men make notes in a personal reading journal. Others use note cards, or write comments on a piece of paper that is inserted in the book. Certainly there are many methods to read with profit, many of which can be excellent. The essential thing is to use one of them.

It is not rare to find men in whom we note an extreme spiritual and intellectual indigence despite the amazing quantity of books they have "devoured." Even though they may have read a lot, they did not know how to read well.

The good reader knows how to discern fundamental books whose wisdom should be assimilated little by little, like the bee distills honey, from books that are for pastime reading. He also recognizes and avoids those books that contain the deadly venom of immorality or bad doctrine, at times disguised by a captivating style or academic theme. Such books should be vigorously avoided. The pretended right of intellectual curiosity regarding certain doctrines is only the false claim of evil, because immorality or bad doctrine lead to our spiritual and intellectual ruin, and not an ennobling life.

When the man arrives at the eve of his life, he looks back retrospectively over his existence. How many good books he intended to read but did not for lack of time! So, take advantage of the time you have while you are still young. Make a reading list of good books and begin to read them. Economize your time and avoid wasting it by reading the many trivial and frivolous books and magazines that abound today. Also do not waste your time watching endless adventure or science fiction movies that rarely benefit the mind or soul.

Books are like friends, it is better to have a few good friends than many superficial acquaintances. You do not need to read many books, but rather some good ones with essential doctrine. These books should be read slowly and meditated upon. A hasty reading, like a quick rain, does not soak the ground or offer a real relief for the mind.

Cultivating an agreeable speech

At times in life occasions will arise when a man must read in public. It is not an easy task. Indeed, it is sad to hear men with many titles embarrass themselves by reading a text poorly, at times their own words.

From early years, the young man should practice reading aloud. He should aim to read not just for himself, but also for the one who hears. With practice, he will stop running together syllables or cutting off the ends of words. He will breathe at the commas, not losing the sense of that beautiful long phrase. He will not be overly dramatic or excessively monotonous. Such readings are tiresome for listeners, who find relief only when they have ended.

In general Americans have the tendency to speak too fast, running together words and slurring syllables. If a young man has bad habits like these, he will need to practice enunciation, carefully pronouncing words, clearly sounding the consonants and vowels. Such exercises can immensely improve one's speaking skills.

Today, with so many technical resources, there are many tools that can assist in the preparation of a reading or a speech. For example, you can xerox and enlarge the pages of the text you intend to read, and then clearly mark the places to pause and breathe in each paragraph. You can also indicate the words you have a tendency to mispronounce or the syllables you want to emphasize. It is a good practice to ask a friend to listen to a rehearsal of your reading and request him to correct your defects. Or you can simply record your reading or speech and listen to the tape to observe where you need to improve.

When the time comes to deliver your speech or reading, place the book or manuscript under a good light without any glare. The reader should know how to follow the lines of the page, staying a little ahead of the words he speaks. He should express himself in a clear, pleasant voice, articulating each word firmly without shouting, pausing slightly at punctuation marks, taking short breaths at the end of phrases. He should make every effort to think about what he is reading in order to establish a good contact with the listeners.

The good orator is one who is an excellent reader. Repeated exercises of reading prepare him for the adept use of the word. To be an orator is not a common talent, because eloquence, like poetry and musical inspiration, are special and rare gifts. Nonetheless, every man with a medium education can be a conference speaker.

Free us, O God, from bad conference speakers...

In times past, a conference speaker was a rare plant, thriving only in university halls, congressional assemblies, and church pulpits. It used to be rare to see someone dare to face the public and tell it what he was thinking. Today, however, with the rapid expanse of media and the modern mania for the spontaneous interview, almost everyone speaks in public at some time or another. This has brought a new scourge to society: Everyone speaks about everything and nothing, without competence or art. We see countless marionettes appear on stage to solicit the tired attention of patient audiences.

The well-bred man does not fear to deliver a speech, but neither does he do so more often than necessary.

It is common in our days to hear an orator speak of himself, his experiences, and his feelings. It is also common to hear a man publicly declare his faults and defects. This is the bad fruit of the Protestant habit of making public confessions. The Modernists and Progressivists feed this tendency by pretending that everyone receives divine revelations and needs to share them with others. With so many people eager to give their personal testimonies, the quality of speeches has fallen almost to the degree the quantity has soared.

The Catholic cultured man avoids such public confessions or personal testimonies. He should speak about principles, historical personages worthy of imitation, or any other topic but himself. He may include an interesting personal anecdote in his talk, but his first aim is to offer facts or insights that reflect the ideas he espouses.

The efficacy of good books

These stories demonstrate the value of reading good books.

From the reading of Sacred Scripture, St. Augustine was moved to turn toward the Catholic Faith. One day he heard about how two officials in the service of the Emperor had both converted and embraced the monastic life after reading the life of St. Anthony of the Desert. This shook him profoundly and gave him the desire to imitate them. At last, the reading of a sentence from the Epistles of St. Paul – "Let us walk honestly, as in the day; not in rioting and drunkenness, not in chambering and wantónness, not in strife and envying" (Rom 13:13) – was the final jolt of grace that wrenched him from his errors and placed him on his knees before God.

St. Ignatius of Loyola was a courageous noble officer who dreamed of human glory. During a long recuperation from a battle wound in the Castle of Loyola, in boredom he picked up a book on the lives of the Saints. He became engrossed in the reading and resolved to follow their example.

One day, to placate his wife after one of his passionate outbursts occasioned by a petty domestic upset, Blessed John Columbini (1300-1367) took up a biography of St. Mary of Egypt. Reading this book was the root of the complete transformation of his life.

When St. Joseph of Cupertino was asked by the Bishop what had inspired his fervor and love for God, he responded that listening to the reading in the refectory of the lives of the Saints had moved him profoundly, and led him to resolve to imitate them.

St Teresa of Avila said that when she was a child, pious readings had awakened in her a desire for martyrdom. Later, books of piety fed and increased her fervor. It was after reading the letters of St. Jerome that she resolved to enter the religious life and joined the Carmelite Order.

One day, St. Pierre Acarie came upon his wife Marie absorbed in the reading of a frivolous novel. He returned to the room carrying a load of pious books and forbid her to read any others until she had finished those. She obeyed. In a short time, she found herself completely transformed. She came to exercise a strong and salutary influence on the Paris of her times. Widowed, she entered the Carmel at Amiens, France in 1613. After her death, the Church raised her to the altar under the name of Blessed Mary of the Incarnation.

St. Jerome related a vision that had a very salutary influence on the rest of his life in a letter to Eustochium, the daughter of St. Paula. It was at the time when he had just entered religious life in a monastery near Antioch. He was indisposed to study the Sacred Books and read them very little. On the contrary, he delighted in the elegance of the profane classical authors and he spent his time reading the works of Cicero, Plato, and Virgil.

One night during Lent in 375, he was transported in spirit before the tribunal of God. The Judge asked him who he was. He answered, "I am a Christian."

"You lie,' replied the Judge. "You are a Ciceronian, for where your treasure is, there also is your heart." And he gave the order that he should be beaten. Jerome begged for divine clemency, which was granted after he promised to no longer read the worldly books.

This was, in fact, no vain and insignificant dream. The Doctor of the Church told Eustochium: "At the hour of waking, I felt quite strongly that it was a reality, for I felt on my shoulders the blows that I had received. Since then, I have read the Holy Scriptures with an even greater ardor than I had for the profane books."